# The Evangelical Revival

# introductions to history

Series Editor: David Birmingham
*Professor of Modern History, University of Kent at Canterbury*

A series initiated by members of the School of History at the University of Kent at Canterbury

*Published titles*

David Birmingham
*The decolonization of Africa*

Christine Bolt
*Feminist ferment: "The woman question" in the USA and England, 1870–1940*

G. M. Ditchfield
*The Evangelical Revival*

Jacqueline Eales
*Women in early modern England*

Doreen Rosman
*From Catholic to Protestant: religion and the people in Tudor England*

Kevin Ruane
*War and revolution in Vietnam*

Bruce Webster
*The Wars of the Roses*

*Forthcoming titles*

David Birmingham
*The Atlantic Empires, 1400–1600*

S-M. Grant
*The American Civil War*

Oonagh Walsh
*Ireland's independence*

David Welch
*Hitler*

# The Evangelical Revival

G. M. Ditchfield
*University of Kent at Canterbury*

First published in 1998 by UCL Press

UCL Press Limited
1 Gunpowder Square
London EC4A 3DE
UK

and

1900 Frost Road, Suite 101
Bristol
Pennsylvania 19007-1598
USA

The name of University College London (UCL) is a registered
trade mark used by UCL Press with the consent of the owner.

**British Library Cataloguing in Publication Data**
A catalogue record for this book is available from the British Library.

ISBN: 1-85728-481-X PB

Typeset in Sabon and Gill Sans by
Acorn Bookwork, Salisbury, Wilts.
Printed and bound by TJ International, Padstow, UK.

# Contents

Preface                                                              vii

Introduction                                                           1

1. The international dimension                                          9

2. Problems and definitions: the British context                      24

3. Revival and the existing British churches                          39

4. The growth of Methodism                                            57

5. Evangelicalism and authority in the late
   eighteenth and early nineteenth centuries                          78

6. The wider impact of the Evangelical Revival                        98

Conclusion                                                           113

Glossary                                                             118

Select bibliography                                                  121

Index                                                                131

To the memory of my parents

# Preface

An attempt to analyze the Evangelical Revival in a work of some 45,000 words is to undergo a lesson in humility of the sort which would have been familiar to many evangelical converts. Much has been omitted; much has been elided and at times over-generalization no doubt seems excessive. Above all, a heavy dependence on the research of others will be obvious and one hopes that justice of a sort has been done to that research. It cannot be emphasized too strongly that this is an introductory guide, designed to encourage readers to embark upon further investigation.

Reasons of space partly explain the British emphasis of the work, although another factor is the priority given to the needs of a British readership. But an attempt has been made to escape from an exclusively Anglo-centric approach and the use of British evidence might best be regarded as a detailed case study rather than a belief that the Revival was confined to the British Isles.

Following conventional (though not universal) usage, the term 'Evangelical' with a capital E has been used to signify a particular way of thought within the Church of England; the term 'evangelical' with a small 'e' signifies that way of thought more generally. I have tried to avoid frequent use of the term as the first word of a sentence. On the other hand, the expression 'Evangelical Revival' with the opening letters in upper case indicates the phenomenon, or series of phenomena, in general.

I am grateful to Margaret Bee, William Gibson, Doreen Rosman, Stephen Taylor and John Walsh for valuable criticism of a preliminary draft. Dr Walsh most kindly allowed me to consult the unpublished manuscript of his work on Calvinism in the Church of England in the age of George III. Trish Hatton gave invaluable help in preparing the final version for publication.

# Introduction

Few parts of the world have been unaffected by the Evangelical Revival of the eighteenth and early nineteenth centuries. Its advocates rarely failed to make some kind of impression. They regularly elicited three types of response: some degree of eager interest which involved significant numbers of conversions; repressive counter-measures which amounted to an implicit tribute to their effectiveness; and a sense of threat among their competitors which led to a renewal of devotional zeal, or at least an attempt to reform abuses, among those competitors. At times, of course, the three responses overlapped. In each case the sense that a phenomenon, welcome, dangerous or curious, was occurring, was a common factor. That sense was justified by the enduring nature of the evangelical phenomenon. Numerous Protestant Churches still describe themselves formally as 'evangelical', while the term has also been used to describe a party, or a way of thought, within Churches which do not use the term in their official titles. In 1970 there was formed a body styled 'Conservative Evangelicals in Methodism' and in 1983 the 'Church of England Evangelical Council' was set up, while the ability of evangelicalism to cross denominational boundaries was seen in the emergence of the National Assembly of Evangelicals in 1965 (Bebbington, 1989: 270). In the United States the National Association of Evangelicals represented thirty denominations with 1,300,000 members in 1947.

The number of books written about evangelicalism, moreover, continues to grow at an ever-increasing rate. A particularly weighty contribution in 1995 was *The Blackwell Dictionary of*

1

*Evangelical Biography 1730–1860,* a two volume compendium of more than 3,500 individual evangelicals, mainly from the English-speaking countries and covering at least four generations. A year earlier, *The Australian Dictionary of Evangelical Biography,* published by the Evangelical History Society in Sydney, provided eloquent testimony to the expansion of evangelicalism beyond its original European, British and North American bases. There is ample evidence in academic journals and university theses of a continuing interest both in the doctrines and in the history of evangelicalism, while the enduring popularity of the biographical genre has generated innumerable lives of evangelical heroes (and heroines). As with many historical movements, enquiry and publication have been stimulated by a consciousness and exploitation of anniversaries. The births and deaths of the famous are prime examples, as are other, perhaps less-noticed, anniversaries. The bicentenary in 1996 of the formal recognition by the Wesleyan Methodist conference of the Circuit Local Preachers' Meeting, for instance, was celebrated by the publication of *Workaday Preachers. The Story of Methodist Local Preaching,* edited by G. Milburn and M. Batty.

The term 'evangelical' has acquired an almost universal currency. Its primary meanings in the *Oxford English Dictionary* are given as 'Of or pertaining to the Gospel' and 'of or pertaining to the Gospel narrative, or to the four Gospels'. Hence, when the eponymous heroine of Charlotte Bronte's *Jane Eyre* (1848) acknowledged the 'evangelical charity' of her rescuer, the clergyman St John Rivers, she would have been understood immediately to mean a duty directly inspired by the gospels to help the less fortunate. Admittedly the term has acquired less favourable connotations in more recent periods. In some quarters, evangelicalism has become associated, perhaps unfairly, with a narrow and intolerant refusal to accept theological innovation or to adapt traditional doctrines to scientific or social change. In the 1920s, in response to theories of evolution which contradicted the account of the creation in the book of Genesis, an evangelical insistence on the literal truth of the Bible helped to divide most of the Protestant Churches in the United States between 'Fundamentalist' and 'Modernist' groups (Cross and Livingstone 1974: 542).

Although the term 'fundamentalist' dates from 1920 and was

used specifically of a group of militantly conservative Protestant groups in the United States, it has since been applied more widely. The association of 'fundamentalism' in world religions with intolerance and even militancy has probably harmed the reputation of evangelicalism, particularly in liberal intellectual circles. Indeed, some evangelicals deny that they are fundamentalist. Similarly, the image of 'revival', or 'revivalism' has been somewhat tarnished by an element of charlatanry, exploitation of the gullible and self-advancement. Sinclair Lewis, in his brilliant depiction of *Elmer Gantry* (1927), presented in fiction the unpleasantly manipulative behaviour of the ego-maniac which could shelter behind the apparent emotionalism of the revivalist preacher: 'To move people – Golly! He wanted to be addressing somebody or something right now, and being applauded!' (ch. 4). The unfavourable impression has lasted, ably assisted by the behaviour of more than a few of Elmer's real-life successors. By contrast, the expression 'Awakening' has not been so discredited and has been applied nearly as much as 'revival' to the events discussed in this book.

These expressions, and the ways in which their meanings have subtly altered over time, make their definition in contemporary context essential. Hence the first two chapters of this book seek to provide precise definitions of 'evangelical' and the quasi-synonymous expressions with which it was coupled, which were understood by contemporaries who applied it to, or were happy to have it applied to, themselves. Historians are perhaps best equipped to explain evangelical beliefs if they rely on first-hand testimony, balancing the views of evangelicals themselves against those of their opponents and those of relatively detached observers. Similarly, their interpretations of a highly complex phenomenon are likely to be most convincing if they place the series of movements of which that phenomenon was composed in the widest possible context. The present study, therefore, needs to explain and justify its approach to the evangelical revival under four types of heading: the geographical, the chronological, the biographical and the denominational.

In terms of geography, the sharpest warning against too narrowly national an approach has been issued by W.R. Ward. His complaint that 'John Wesley may have claimed that the world

3

was his parish, but Methodist historians have been strongly tempted to make his parish their world' (Ward 1980: 231) amounts to an injunction to look far beyond English shores. It is essential to appreciate that evangelicalism was trans-national and trans-continental. Chapter one of this book discusses the central European developments of the later seventeenth and early eighteenth centuries to assess the extent to which they anticipated the rise of those movements which are inextricably linked in the minds of English-speaking readers with John Wesley. An exclusively English approach is inappropriate on at least two grounds. It fails to take account of the vital contribution of continental Protestantism and the dramatic stirrings in North American Congregationalism associated with Jonathan Edwards. By regarding 'England' as synonymous with 'Britain', moreover, it ignores or marginalizes the development of evangelicalism in Scotland, Wales and Ireland. In each of the three kingdoms and the principality the revival took different forms and only by treating each in its own right can full advantage be taken of the excellent research dealing specifically with each. A 'four nations' approach to what was once 'English' history has been exemplified by Linda Colley in *Britons* and it is particularly appropriate for a study of evangelicalism. The major individuals of the revival became genuinely international figures. The existence of an increasingly effective print culture permitted the growth of a sophisticated system of communication, by means of which information about evangelical movements was transmitted rapidly from country to country and continent to continent. The central years of the revival, moreover, coincided with (and perhaps helped to stimulate) considerable imperial expansion and missionary endeavour. Hence the extra-European dimension is also one that cannot be overlooked.

In terms of chronology it is certainly true that the Evangelical Revival has come to be associated with key dates. Of these, probably the most celebrated is 24 May 1738 when John Wesley, according to his own account, experienced a conversion which perhaps was second only to that of St Paul in terms of its wider significance. To that date could be added the expulsion of the Oxford Methodists in 1768, the split within Methodism in 1795–6 and the defeat of Lord Sidmouth's bill in 1811. Specific events such as these are of undeniable importance. But the dates mentioned above not only have a rather Anglo-centric appearance. An excessive concentration upon them also has the effect of over-emphasizing the short term at the expense of the long term. The Revival was a process which can be traced back to the late seventeenth century; which had even earlier antecedents; and which retains a presence in the present day world. Hence, although the main focus of this book will be the century between 1730 and 1830, frequent reference will of necessity be made to earlier and later periods. The famous events of the 1730s did not spring from nothing. Although a conscious search for 'origins' is open to accusations of a whiggish present-mindedness, the Revival cannot be explained without proper consideration of broader historical tendencies in the Europe of Louis XIV, William III and Augustus II of Saxony at the end of the seventeenth century.

The third approach concerns the roles of individuals and of their followers. There has been, and still is, a tendency to view the revival through the lives of great men. It was a tendency which began with the revival itself and which the revival encouraged. From their Puritan forebears evangelicals drew the practice of regular (and sometimes painful) spiritual self-examination which often took the form of autobiography. Such autobiographies were often published, as were biographies of the leading figures, which quickly spawned an iconography of portrait and statue. It was understandable that a highly personal religion should be perceived historically in personal terms. Although individual leaders are of undoubted importance, this process has, perhaps, been taken too far. Sympathizers tended to attribute the revival almost exclusively to the working of the grace of God through inspired individuals. In an emotional sermon preached at the funeral of John Wesley on 9 March 1791, John Whitehead declared:

If we consider the state of these kingdoms, when the two Mr WESLEY'S and Mr WHITEFIELD first went out to preach publicly, we must acknowledge that experimental religion was almost lost, at least among the common people ... What were you, O ye Methodists, before you heard these three servants of God, and those associated with them declare the glad tidings of peace and salvation? You were scattered in the world, ignorant of God, and of the things that belong to your peace and salvation: but you that were not a people, are now become the people of God, by their instrumentality (Whitehead 1791: 50–1).

In the same year the political writer and memoirist Horace Walpole, a less friendly commentator, offered a similar interpretation when he noted that John Wesley and the Countess of Huntingdon had died within a few months of each other. 'The patriarchess of the Methodists ... is dead', he wrote, 'Now she and Whitefield and Wesley are gone, the sect will probably decline: a second crop of apostles seldom acquire the influence of the founders' (Lewis 1937–83: 11, p. 297). The inaccuracy of this forecast not only reminds us to take account of that second generation but enforces the lesson that the successes of evangelicalism rested to a large extent upon its rank and file. Hence recent research into the social composition of the vital evangelical groups will be deployed to illustrate the levels of society from which their adherents were mainly drawn. The individual clergyman, patron, lay preacher, member and irregular listener all demand attention and the existence in print of large numbers of obituaries, autobiographies and memoirs have permitted something of a prosopographical, or method of 'collective biography', to be adopted by some historians. The clergy have frequently received most attention because their relatively high social background and superior education make them the easiest to trace, through family histories, their own published work and the annals of their schools and universities. But it is vital to focus on the laity of evangelicalism as well. Such a method allows for the introduction of a theme which has been for too long neglected, namely the active participation of women in evangelical movements. It was not until 1992 that the Methodist Publishing House reprinted Zechariah Taft's two-volume *Biographical Sketches of the Lives of various Holy Women*, which first appeared in 1825–8.

Fourthly, this book recognizes the unsuitability of a strictly denominational approach to evangelicalism. For all the attention rightly accorded to the various forms of Methodism, the largest single branch of the stream, a history of evangelicalism is a history of ideas which influenced virtually every Protestant sect or denomination. Moreover, evangelicalism has always carried within it an impulse towards a non-doctrinal unity of Christians based on a small core of basic biblical propositions. Its thrust towards cross-denominational co-operation has fed into twentieth-century ecumenicalism and A.J. Lewis subtitled his biography of Count Zinzendorf (1962) 'The ecumenical pioneer'. Although this book devotes a chapter to Methodism, it also gives full consideration to other evangelical groups, notably the Moravians and other sects which had their origins in central Europe, as well as the Evangelical elements within the Church of England and the evangelical re-invigoration of much of the older Protestant nonconformity in Britain.

After an opening chapter which seeks to provide the essential international context, therefore, the second chapter moves to the British Isles. The evidence from so wide an area should make possible a definition of evangelicalism which takes full account of its regional diversities as well as its common characteristics. At this point it will be appropriate to consider the affinities (and differences) between evangelicalism and what are often assumed to have been the secularizing influences of the European enlightenment. The third chapter takes this theme further by exploring the early stages of the revival in Britain and Ireland, with particular reference to its Welsh, Scottish and Irish forms, as well as to the more familiar story of the Oxford Holy Club and the involvement of the Moravians. From such a background, it will be possible to concentrate in the fourth chapter upon the social, religious and political factors which facilitated the growth of Methodism, as well as the obstacles and hostility which it faced. The tensions within evangelicalism in general and within Methodism in particular will form the subject of the fifth chapter. It focuses upon the later eighteenth and early nineteenth centuries, when the possibilities of clashes with the state loomed large and when evangelicalism was obliged to respond to the challenge of revolution in Europe and North America. The final chapter stands back somewhat from the preceding narrative to comment on the methods by which the revival was propagated and on the popularization of its ideas. It then discusses the role of women within the movement and the ways in which evangelicalism influenced, challenged or reinforced many of the fundamental assumptions of traditional society; this will involve a brief discussion of reform movements and campaigns for the 'refinement' of manners.

One is conscious that some theological and other terms which were familiar to contemporaries are less so to the reader who is making initial acquaintance with the subject. Accordingly a brief glossary of such terms is provided at the end of this book.

# CHAPTER ONE

# The international dimension

Evangelicalism was the principal feature of the Protestant world in the eighteenth and nineteenth centuries. Its origins in Germany, Britain and North America, though far from identical, had important features in common. The characteristics which it developed make international generalizations possible, and those generalizations apply to other areas to which it was communicated, notably to British colonies in India, Australasia and the Caribbean. Its geographical extent was such that it cannot be attributed purely to national or local factors. Although it took different forms in different societies, the evangelical revival is best regarded as a series of separately-generated but none the less interdependent international events. Indeed, evangelicalism placed so heavy a stress upon the duty of seeking to save souls by preaching and by missionary endeavour that it could hardly be confined to one community, one state or even one continent.

It has become conventional to regard the 1730s as the decade during which the continental European, the North American and the British revivals began. This was the decade in which Count Zinzendorf in Saxony, Jonathan Edwards in Northampton, Massachusetts, Howell Harris in South Wales and the Wesley brothers and George Whitefield in England launched the campaigns which achieved such celebrity. However, recent work by W.R. Ward has located the origin of many of the religious characteristics which came to be termed 'evangelical' in central and eastern Germany at a somewhat earlier period, at the end of the seventeenth and the very beginning of the eighteenth century. Hence it is necessary to examine the religious condition of Europe at the time when the

9

celebrated individuals mentioned above were born, rather than when they came to maturity.

The second half of the seventeenth century in Europe was the high point of the Counter-Reformation. It was an age of Catholic recovery and resurgence. Of course in parts of southern Europe the Catholic Church had remained virtually unchallenged. Protestantism made no progress in Spain, Portugal or Italy, and it is not surprising that these areas tend to be absent from histories of evangelicalism. But in other areas the Catholic Church appeared to be advancing. The Austrian Habsburgs pushed back the invasions of the Ottoman Turks and began to re-conquer Hungary for Catholicism. More significantly, however, the Catholic Church appeared to be in the process of reversing the verdicts of the Reformation and of the Thirty Years' War. Although the Treaty of Westphalia (1648) had provided legal recognition for the Protestant rulers of German states, in the succeeding half-century several of those states acquired Catholic rulers. In 1685, for instance, the formerly Protestant Palatinate of the Rhine was inherited by a branch of the strongly Catholic Wittelsbach family of Bavaria. In southern Germany, Austria and Switzerland the triumphalism of the Counter-Reformation was powerfully expressed in visual form by the ornate Baroque churches with their distinctive onion-shaped domes. Many of them proclaimed their Jesuit origins with their dedications to St Francis Xavier, reminding those who saw them that the Jesuit Order was one of the spearheads of the post-Tridentine Catholic Church. The Revocation of the Edict of Nantes by Louis XIV in 1685 forced much of the Protestant, or Huguenot, minority in France, into exile. This was Catholicism at its most flamboyant and expansionist and the effect upon European Protestantism was dramatic.

Not only did beleaguered Protestant minorities face the likelihood of persecution under hostile Catholic regimes but there seemed a serious danger to Protestant states themselves. While in 1580 almost half of Europe had been Protestant, by 1700 that proportion had been reduced to only about one-fifth. The Protestant states were confined to the northern and north western fringes of Western Europe and there seemed to be every prospect that they would be pushed back even further. In 1719 there was serious danger of a religious civil war in Germany (Ward 1980:

234), while international support for Jacobite rebellions threatened to bring about a restoration of the Catholic Stuart family in vehemently-Protestant Britain.

A combination of increased repression within Catholic monarchies and what appeared to be a process of Catholic encroachment upon Protestant states led to an understandable sense of crisis on the part of European Protestantism. Traditional Protestant depictions of the Catholic Church as intolerant, persecuting and corrupt were reinforced. Such depictions were rapidly communicated through the testimony of refugees, through print and through the visual image. One should not underestimate the extent to which the evangelical revival derived succour from a strong sense of anti-Catholicism, a sense which it retained well into the twentieth century. It helps to explain why the revival largely took the form of a process whereby Protestants converted other Protestants or the previously irreligious to another form of Protestantism and why the revival made little if any direct impression upon European Catholicism.

In Ward's view the most important Catholic advance took place in 1697, when the wealthy and strategically important Protestant state of Saxony passed under Catholic rule. Its elector, Frederick Augustus II, was chosen to succeed to the vacant (and elective) throne of Poland and converted to Catholicism as a condition of doing so. Saxony, the homeland of Martin Luther and one of the cradles of the sixteenth-century Reformation, found itself under what threatened to be alien government. There was also criticism within Saxony itself of what was allegedly the excessively dry, formal and rigid worship of the orthodox Lutheran Church which, in the Electorate, was the dominant form of religion. It was depicted as narrowly scholastic, socially exclusive and remote from ordinary people. Hence at the popular level, the Lutheran Churches of Saxony (and elsewhere) seemed to be in no position to resist the perceived threat from an advancing Catholicism.

Much of this criticism emanated from that group of German Protestants known as Pietists. Though not easy to define, the term denotes a highly personal form of religion, with a strong emphasis on the individual's direct relationship with God and the need for a 'New Birth' to cement that relationship. Its principal spokesman – and, according to some authorities its founder – was Philipp

Jakob Spener (1635–1705). Whereas orthodox Lutheranism in Saxony gave priority to outward observance through official institutions, Pietism stressed the individual's inward experience acquired independently of those institutions. Although born in Alsace and with a distinguished pastoral reputation as a Lutheran minister in Strasbourg and Frankfurt, it was Spener's appointment as court chaplain to the Elector of Saxony at Dresden that made him a figure of international importance. He introduced in Saxony the characteristics of Pietism which were to be among the hallmarks also of early evangelicalism. The Pietists promoted a domestic approach to religion which refused to confine itself to formal church services. Spener organized a series of class meetings, often in private houses, in which those who took part reviewed their religious conduct, provided mutual support and encouraged each other in biblical and devotional reading. He was neither a theological innovator nor a separatist; he promulgated no new (or 'heretical') doctrine and had no ambitions to become the charismatic leader of a breakaway movement. As Professor Ward puts it, he offered 'not a protest movement of the "spiritualist" or quakerish kind, but a response from within the church to a perceived spiritual need' (Ward 1992: 58). However, the implication that those who had experienced the 'New Birth', whatever their social status, were entitled – indeed obliged – to preach it carried a potential challenge to the authority of the established clergy. Male and female servants as well as artisans had attended Spener's class meetings at Frankfurt (Ward 1992: 57). By proclaiming the 'priesthood of all believers', Spener and his associates, notably August Hermann Francke (1663–1727) of the university of Leipzig, were – however indirectly – introducing a quasi-democratic element into their religious proceedings. Such an element had been present in later medieval heretical movements and, more recently, among English Puritans, whose devotional literature had been well received in Germany. Invariably it led to political controversy.

The official response to Pietism in Saxony is revealing. The Lutheran churches in the German states were far from uniform in their devotional practices. In parts of the Rhineland and elsewhere the prevailing tendency of Lutheranism was of a 'reformed' type, involving a more thorough repudiation of Catholic practices (such as confession) and the acceptance of a greater degree of lay initiative than in Saxony, where the Lutheran church was more resistant to innovation. In particular, in the universities of Wittenberg and Leipzig there was a sincerely-held fear that a combination of an active piety and lay participation would lead to religious excess and schism. It will be evident that such fears were expressed, and often acted upon, wherever evangelicalism subsequently appeared.

By 1692 Spener, Francke and their associates had been expelled from Saxony. But, not for the first or last time in the history of religion, an expulsion had considerable international effect. The Pietists quickly found refuge and succour in the adjacent territory of Brandenburg-Prussia, a rising power in north Germany, whose ruler, the Hohenzollern Frederick I, was elevated from the status of Elector to that of monarch in 1701. Prussia, too, was a Protestant state, anxious about a Catholic threat and in a state of rivalry with the Austrian Habsburgs, who had been the principal Catholic champions in the Thirty Years' War. The Habsburg family had come almost to monopolize the title and prestige, together with the ecclesiastical patronage, of Holy Roman Emperor. The Prussian monarchy also regarded Saxony as a rival, initially for the leadership of the Protestant states of Germany, latterly as a potentially hostile Catholic power with the conversion of Augustus II and his accession to the Polish crown. In Prussia, moreover, the bulk of the population adhered to a less rigid form of Lutheranism than that officially promulgated in Saxony. Accordingly, the Pietist exiles were well received and, not unlike Huguenot refugees in England and elsewhere at exactly the same time, were perceived as an asset to the state. Spener became Rector of the Nikolaikirche at Berlin, while Francke was made a professor, first of oriental languages, then of theology, at the newly-founded (July 1694) university of Halle and pastor of the nearby parish of Glauchau.

Halle merits special consideration in the history of the Evangelical Revival. Situated as it was in the Prussian-controlled territory of Magdeburg, it rapidly acquired a reputation as a kind of early headquarters of reformed and outgoing Protestantism. It was the birthplace of George Frideric Handel (1685–1759), an appropriate piece of symbolism in view of the centrality of music in the revival and Handel's later role as the trumpeter of the Protestant succession in Hanoverian Britain. Halle was an industrial town of considerable economic and strategic importance. Over and above that, however, its new university became a remarkable intellectual centre, with high prestige attaching to its medical, law and theological faculties. It drew scholars from all over Europe and beyond; Halle is believed to have been the first university to have admitted an African. It has been described as 'a powerhouse of early Enlightenment thinking' (Geyer-Kordesch 1994: 311). The theology faculty was dominated by Pietists. Under Francke's leadership they were able to advocate the personal nature of Christianity and to involve the laity in biblical exploration. They were opposed, it is true, by elements among the orthodox Lutheran clergy but, as had not been the case in Saxony, they benefited from royal favour and protection. Most significant of all was the philanthropic work to which Francke devoted the rest of his life.

Francke's main legacy was the construction of a series of schools and orphanages which combined a charitable and an educational purpose. The 'Waisenhaus', or orphanage, which he established in 1696 provided pupils for the university and soon attracted large numbers; its residents and staff exceeded 3,000. Whether all its residents were in fact orphans is open to question; what is certain is that Halle as a well-marketed philanthropic institution flourished. Francke was responsible for the education of his charges in the Pietist manner and added a dispensary to his other foundations. Its medical products were advertized in the major European languages and were soon in demand throughout Europe (Ward 1992: 62). Hence finance for these ambitious projects was raised and it was supplemented by charitable appeals. Moreover, since the educational reforms promoted by Francke included practical training for the service of the state, Halle was of considerable value to the Prussian monarchy, which was in the process of developing a substantial army and state bureaucracy and welcomed sources of well-educated recruits for both.

Partly for this reason Francke was able to publish and disseminate his views without official censorship – an unusual condition in the Europe of his time. His printing press issued Bibles and devotional literature on a substantial scale. In what was to become a characteristic feature of evangelicalism (though not something peculiar to it) Francke and his associates provided bible translations and religious literature in the languages of eastern Europe. He sought to spread the Pietist message, particularly to the Protestant minorities in the Catholic territories of the Habsburg empire. Silesia, Lusatia, Hungary and Bohemia were among Francke's targets and he succeeded in establishing a mission at the strategic town of Teschen, from where easy physical access to all these territories could be obtained. Francke's aspiration to 'create a second Halle at Teschen' (Ward 1992: 63) was unsuccessful, but his wider objective of communicating his ideas was more than fulfilled. He published a newspaper, the thrice-weekly *Hallesche Zeitung*, from 1708, at much the same time as the first daily newspaper in England, the *Daily Courant*, appeared in 1702. He also communicated by means of an astonishingly large private correspondence. It has been estimated that altogether he had some 5,000 correspondents and that he remained in contact with 300–400 of them on a regular basis (Ward 1992: 2). Pietism found a response in the south-western German state of Wurttemberg, where its leading figure, Johannes Albrecht Bengel (1687–1752) is credited with having written some 1,200 letters per year (Ward 1992: 2). In Wurttemberg, too, one finds the same private meetings for prayer and self-examination, together with Bengel's own contribution of millenarianism. His textual researches into the New Testament convinced him that the second coming of Christ upon earth could be predicted with total certainty for the year 1836. The element of millenarianism in the Evangelical Revival, thought not shared by all its exponents, should not be overlooked. Bengel was far from the only writer to engage in millenarian expectations. His specific prediction, however, became known and was discussed in England. The *Public Advertiser* of 19 June 1788, along with other newspapers, published a letter from John Wesley to one of his lay preachers in which he dissociated himself from the prophecy.

It is a central argument of Professor Ward's work that many of the characteristics of the British and American revivals had been anticipated in late seventeenth-century Germany and in seventeenth-century Scotland. He refers particularly to camp-meetings, field preaching, class-meetings and informal domestic piety, together with the circulation of classics of Reformation literature (Ward 1980: 239, 248). Certainly the international dimensions of

15

the Pietist movements at Halle and elsewhere are undeniable. They were reinforced by what may be termed, without exaggeration, a diaspora of Protestant refugees in early eighteenth-century Europe. Most of them sought to escape from that sense of Catholic encroachment and persecution to which reference has been made. They included Huguenots escaping from France after the revocation of the Edict of Nantes in 1685; refugees fleeing the Palatinate of the Rhine during the war of the Spanish Succession; emigrants from Silesia (a Habsburg possession until its conquest by Prussia in the 1740s), Poles and Slovaks. The most dramatic and startling episodes of migration, however, were those which involved the Moravians and the Salzburgers and each requires slightly more detailed treatment.

One of the ways in which the Pietist message reached a wider audience was through Spener's godson, Nikolaus Ludwig, Count von Zinzendorf. His importance lies partly in his aristocratic status and personal wealth; his family owned substantial estates in lower Saxony and their patronage was bound to be of considerable assistance to a religious group which found favour with them. Zinzendorf was, as his biographer puts it, 'cradled in religion' (Lewis 1962: 21). His mother was a fervent Pietist and he himself was educated partly at Francke's school at Halle. He developed a strong sense of personal religion, a personal relationship with Christ which involved an impulse towards sacrifice, asceticism and service in return for the sacrifice of Christ which, Zinzendorf believed, had secured the forgiveness and salvation of those who would recognize the fact and act accordingly. His independent means allowed him the opportunity for travel and his visits to Holland and France brought him into contact with other groups of Protestants. Partly because of such connections he began to add to his Pietist convictions a zeal for an active, preaching ministry which would supplement the printed word propagated by Halle with an international network of missionaries. His interest in missionary work was made possible by his acquaintance with the Moravians, a group which, despite its smallness of numbers, appears and re-appears repeatedly in the early history of the Revival.

The Moravian Church has a legitimate claim to be the oldest Protestant Church in Europe. Its origins lie in the Bohemian reform movement of the early fifteenth century and its leader, and martyr, John Hus. He was condemned at the Council of Constance and burned at the stake in 1415, but his followers survived and, despite internal divisions, in 1457–8 formed their own formal organization, the 'Unitas Fratrum' (Unity of the Brethren). Their objections to the practices of the Catholic Church were more moral than theological and their ethos took the form of a communitarian way of life, a material simplicity and a degree of unworldiness which repudiated the sophistication and wealth of the higher clergy. There was no intention to break away from the Catholic Church, merely to seek its internal reform. For many decades, indeed, the Bohemian church enjoyed considerable local autonomy and the Brethren spread into Moravia (whence their subsequent name) and Poland. But as the Brethren began to move in what was perceived to be an anti-Catholic direction, and particularly when it became their practice to administer the communion in both kinds to the laity, they incurred increasing official hostility. The latter point was of much political, as well as devotional significance; the Catholic practice had been for the priest alone to take the wine as the symbol of Christ's blood. For the laity to be so directly involved in this ceremony was another example of that quasi-democratic ethos which caused anxiety both to the ecclesiastical and secular authorities.

The subsequent history of the Brethren was one of alternating periods of persecution and slight relaxation. The rulers of Bohemia, the Austrian Habsburgs, regarded them with increasing suspicion, especially at times of religious warfare, when their reluctance to serve in the armed forces gave them the appearance of subversives. Their fortunes reached their lowest points during European conflicts. The early stages of the Thirty Years' War in the 1620s resulted in the persecution, and virtual extinction, of the Brethren in Bohemia and Moravia and the severe reduction of their numbers in Poland. One of their most gifted members, however, Johannes Amos Comenius (1592–1670) achieved celebrity as an educational reformer. His works, advocating what were by the standards of his time fairly libertarian ideals with an aspiration towards a unified Church based on Christian love, helped to give the Brethren an influence far beyond the boundaries of their original settlements. Comenius ended his days in Holland

17

and in the half century after his death the Brethren seemed on the verge of extinction. But at Fulneck in northern Moravia, where Comenius had been minister, a few settlements persisted and at the turn of the century they made contact with the Silesian revival which had been inspired by the Pietists through Francke's outpost at Teschen.

From here in 1722 a small group of Moravian families retreated into southern Saxony and found refuge on Zinzendorf's estate at Berthelsdorf. Led by the carpenter Christian David, an inspirational if excessively impulsive figure, they were allowed to build a new settlement, which they named Herrnhut (the watch of the Lord). At first their skills as artisans helped them to win acceptance by Zinzendorf's steward, but subsequently the Count himself became keenly interested in their history and communitarian ideals. In May 1727, by which time the settlement at Herrnhut numbered 300, he imposed his own authority on the incipient factionalism of the new arrivals, won their acceptance of a regular series of statutes and transformed them from 'a group of quarrelling schismatics to an organized body of orderly Christian tenants' (Hutton 1909: 207). The celebration of Holy Communion on 13 August 1727 set the seal upon the renewal of the Unitas Fratrum, or, as they were increasingly known, the Moravian Brethren. Like their predecessors, and like the Pietists, they had no intention of forming a separate church. As a young man, Zinzendorf had formed a small society called the Order of the Grain of Mustard Seed, with the purpose of stimulating and reinvigorating the existing churches from within. Now his purpose was similar, namely to promote the concept of 'ecclesiolae in Ecclesia' (little churches within the church), that is to say, small and fundamentally loyal pressure groups. The main contribution of the Moravians lay in the field of overseas missions. In 1732 missionaries from Herrnhut departed for the Caribbean islands and in the following year for Greenland. It was not long before converted Eskimos were presented, under Moravian auspices, to King George II in London.

It is true that Zinzendorf subsequently fell foul of the authorities in Saxony, quarrelled even with the more conservative Pietists, and was indeed briefly exiled from the Electorate. His exile, however, encouraged him to travel to Holland, England and

North America to promote the ideals of Herrnhut. During the 1730s Moravian settlements were founded in the Netherlands (Zeist), the Protestant cantons of Switzerland and the Baltic lands. As is explained in the next two chapters, the Moravians also established a presence in Britain.

Meanwhile, however, there had taken place the second key element of the Protestant diaspora, the expulsion of the Salzburgers. In November 1731 the Catholic Archbishop of Salzburg, Leopold Anton Eleutherius von Firmian, ordered the ejection of what he believed to be a subversive but none the less small Lutheran minority from his territory. The Archbishop, a sovereign ruler but a close ally of the Austrian Habsburgs, inherited from his predecessors an ambition to turn Salzburg into an architectural and spiritual rival to Rome as the champion of the Counter-Reformation. But partly as a result of contacts with Moravians and visiting Pietists, Protestant numbers in the archdiocese were far larger than had been anticipated. Many of the Salzburg Protestants were of considerable economic value to the state, including a significant number of coal and salt miners in the remote Defereggertal region. When the enforced emigration of those Protestants, who would not renounce their religion, was effected, more than 20,000 people were involved. The fact that the expulsion took place with the minimum of notice and in the depth of winter added to the sense of martyrdom. It also became known all over Europe and has been described as 'one of the sensations of the eighteenth century' (Ward 1992: 103). Protestant states raised funds for their assistance and accepted them as refugees. Of the emigrants, by far the largest group settled, like the Pietists from Saxony, in Prussia. A smaller number settled, less successfully, in the Netherlands and some 200 reached England where, with the encouragement of the Georgia Trustees, they founded in 1734 a settlement, named in suitably biblical style Ebenezer ('stone of help') near Savannah, Georgia, in Britain's newest North American colony (Ward 1980: 246–7; Jones 1984: 14–36). The Salzburgers shared many of the characteristics of the Pietists and Moravians and their dispersal helped to bring these various groups further into contact with each other. It was in Georgia that the Wesley brothers and George Whitefield began their international missionary work.

The early stages of the revival in the international context were greatly facilitated by the ability of those involved to communicate news of developments from one part of the world to another. This was not an evangelical invention; since the Reformation there had been contacts between Protestants which crossed national and imperial frontiers, while the Puritan emigration to North America and the Presbyterian triumph in Scotland had allowed a 'Calvinist international' to develop, with British, Dutch, French and Swiss involvement. Personal letters and personal contacts made possible by travel were the most obvious means of communication and it is striking to note how many vital developments in the revival were triggered by a meeting between two key figures. 'What would the history of Methodism have been if John Wesley, High Church Anglican, had not met Peter Böhler, a Moravian?' (Walsh 1994: 20). However, the crucial element in the evangelical network of communication was the printed word. It is clear from the work of Susan O'Brien that literacy in its many sub-divisions was essential to the revival and that a religious print culture which was both sophisticated and international was in existence well before the eighteenth century. It took the form of reprinting older material, the circulating of published sermons and tracts and the reproduction of the journals and diaries of the leading protagonists. The autobiographical tendencies of many evangelicals quickly developed; the publication of their journals was intended to have a galvanizing and tonic effect upon their colleagues in other areas and to provide evidence of the success of a divine plan. Between 1738 and 1741 seven volumes of George Whitefield's *Journals*, recording his missionary activities, were issued and because of their direct and accessible style, reached a wide readership (O'Brien 1994: 47). The revival narrative became an important literary genre in its own right, as did evangelical magazines and newsletters, in many cases catering for the popular level. The importance of print culture in transatlantic religious communication in later periods is well known; it helps to explain the ultimate success of anti-slavery movements and the Anglo-American dimension to such philanthropic causes as prison reform. It is important, however, to recognize its existence in earlier periods and not to post-date its origins.

Some of the best examples of such communication were those

which crossed the Atlantic. Protestant emigration to the northern colonies, though predominantly English and Scottish, also included German, Swiss and Scandinavian settlements, notably in Pennsylvania, and a strong Dutch presence in New York. Indeed the Dutch Reformed clergyman Theodorus Jacobus Frelinghuysen, who preached extensively and frequently on an itinerant basis in New York state during the 1720s, is sometimes credited with the initial inspiration of the North American revival. The transatlantic Protestant connection, therefore, was not simply Anglo-American, but also one between continental Europe and America. It applied, moreover, to critics as well as advocates of revival (O'Brien 1994: 46). The result was that events on each side of the Atlantic were widely reported, in both a friendly and hostile manner. There were particularly close links between Scotland and New England. Clergy in both territories at the beginning of the eighteenth century turned from efforts for moral reformation to intense prayers for divine grace in bringing about a religious revival. A belief that the moral reformation of individuals on a substantial scale would itself lead to revival gave way to the view that only a divine outpouring of grace in the form of a revival could produce the desired moral reformation (Crawford 1991: 41–2, 51). When symptoms of revival manifested themselves, they could be interpreted as direct answers to prayers.

At this point, however, it is necessary to emphasize the local and the indigenous in the appearance of specific revivals. The most celebrated name in eighteenth-century American evangelicalism is – rightly – that of Jonathan Edwards (1703–58) Congregational minister at Northampton, Massachusetts. In 1734 Edwards preached a dramatic sermon on the importance of repentance and the immediate dangers of sin to his congregation and rapidly set in motion a series of conversions and emotional experiences which amounted to a revival. In his account of these proceedings, significantly entitled *A Faithful Narrative of the Surprising Work of God in the Conversion of many hundred souls in Northampton* (1737), Edwards gave particular credit to his grandfather, Solomon Stoddard, one of his predecessors at Northampton, who had inspired a small-scale revival in the 1670s. He also emphasized the local roots of the revival with which he was associated. Outside influence, least of all from central Europe, could have little if any effect in a small town as remote as North-ampton:

> Our being so far within the land, at a distance from sea-ports, and in a corner of the country, has doubtless been one reason why we have not been so much corrupted with vice, as most other parts ... We being much separated from other parts of the province, and having comparatively but little intercourse with them, have from the beginning always managed our ecclesiastical affairs within ourselves: 'tis the way in which the county, from its infancy, has gone on, by the practical agreement of all (quoted in Goen (ed.) 1972: 144–5).

Edwards organized evening lectures in 'social religion' for the young. Clearly evoking a strong response in a community where several sudden and apparently inexplicable deaths had occurred, he won numerous conversions in Northampton and the sur-rounding area in the valley of the Connecticut river. He claimed that 'There was scarcely a single person in the town, either old or young, that was left unconcerned about the great things of the eternal world' (quoted in Goen (ed.) 1972: 150). The testimony of six of Edwards's fellow-ministers in the same county was obtained as corroboration of his account.

It should be added that Edwards was not the first to be credited with a revival of this nature and that, in comparison with many later developments, what happened in Northampton was on a small scale. Its broader significance derived from two factors. Firstly, in 1740 the Methodist preacher George Whitefield, who had already acquired an extraordinary popularity as a preacher in Britain, visited New England, drew large crowds and helped to turn Edwards's fairly modest revival into something approximat-ing to the 'Great Awakening' celebrated in American history. Crucially, however, Whitefield came to New England after, and because of, the earlier revival; he did not initiate it. Secondly, the work of Edwards attracted immense international interest in the Protestant world. The *Faithful Narrative* was first published in London in 1737, in an abridged form and with an endorsement by two prominent English Dissenting ministers, Isaac Watts and John

Guyse. The publicity which followed confirmed that the 'revival' was taking a trans-continental form and the interest shown by other evangelicals demonstrates the value they placed upon accounts of success elsewhere. As Edwards himself wrote in the *Faithful Narrative*, 'God has made such a means of promoting his work amongst us, as the news of others' conversion' (quoted in Goen (ed.) 1972: 176).

If the revival in Northampton is explained by primarily local factors then so, perhaps, is its decline. It was criticized for the excessive emotionalism of some of the converts; it fell foul of the authorities in Connecticut; Edwards was severely criticized especially by the Boston clergyman Charles Chauncy, and was removed from his Northampton pastorate in 1749. 'By 1744 the Great Awakening in New England was virtually over' (Ward 1992: 292), although, in different forms, it continued elsewhere. One reason for the controversial nature of Edwards's preaching was his strictly orthodox Calvinism; he saw his conversions as the awakening of God's elect to an appreciation of their own salvation. The question as to whether salvation was open to all, or confined to the divinely-chosen few, was to be a highly contentious one. That the Revival in some areas took a Calvinist and in others an Arminian form was a crucial development and will require further explanation. This is a theme which is examined in some detail in chapter four. For present purposes, however, the contention, sometimes bitter, of Arminian and Calvinist may serve as evidence of the local and regional differences, as well as the similarities, between the revival in widely-separated societies. Those local peculiarities assume even greater importance when we turn to the revival in the British Isles.

# CHAPTER TWO

# Problems and definitions: the British context

It will be apparent from the international context that at least four important characteristics can be detected in the Protestant revival movements so far considered. One is a sense of expectation, possibly induced by external social and political pressures, or by internal theological controversy. A second is the fertile ground for revival that was to be found among persecuted minorities in some Catholic lands. A third feature is the way in which revivals emerged from within the ranks of established or official churches or (in the case of Jonathan Edwards) from a church with quasi-official support that fell short of formal establishment. A fourth feature is the almost complete absence of any intention on the part of the leaders of revival to break away from the parent church and form a breakaway or distinctive sect; in each case the objective was to move the Church itself in a particular direction. Admittedly, that objective often involved severe criticism of the Church by the revivalists. But the ultimate separation, if it occurred, tended to be the result of sustained official attacks upon the revivalists themselves as 'schismatics', leading to their virtual expulsion.

The sense of expectation was undoubtedly heightened by the news of international developments. It is quite possible that the revival in the British Isles, had it occurred at all, would have taken a very different form without the arrival of Huguenots, Moravians and (to a lesser extent) Salzburgers, together with reports of developments in Germany. But there were factors which were peculiar to the British Isles as well, and those factors varied considerably between the three kingdoms and the principality. Those factors are best explored by drawing on contemporary evidence and it is to such evidence that it is necessary to turn in order to define precisely what is meant by the expression 'evangelicalism'. Of its complexity, adaptability and diversity there can be no doubt. But it is important not to allow its complexity to forbid definition altogether. For one crucial aid in forming a definition is the knowledge that the words 'evangelical' and 'Revival' were both frequently written and spoken during the eighteenth century and cannot be discounted as later, anachronistic, terminology invented by historians.

In fact the term evangelical has a long history and was in use well before the start of the eighteenth century. When Dr Samuel Johnson compiled his *Dictionary of the English Language* between 1746 and 1755, he had a double advantage in dealing with the word. There were many pre-eighteenth century examples of its use which he could study, and the eighteenth-century revival in England had proceeded far enough for him to be able to take it into account. He defined 'evangelical' in two senses. The first was 'agreeable to gospel; consonant to the Christian law revealed in the holy gospel', illustrated – significantly, in view of the conclusions of Dr Walsh, discussed below – by two quotations from the sermons of the early eighteenth-century High Churchman Francis Atterbury. The second sense was, more pithily, 'contained in the gospel'. 'Evangelism' he defined as 'the promulgation of the blessed gospel' and 'Evangelist' as 'a writer of the history of our Lord Jesus' (i.e. the authors of the first four books of the New Testament) and 'a promulgator of the Christian laws'. Some of the definitions in Johnson's *Dictionary* were erroneous, controversial or whimsical; these were not. For the crucial term in each of his explications is the word 'gospel'. By definition, evangelicalism denoted the preaching of the gospel, with the emphasis on the message of hope contained in the New Testament.

The full extent to which evangelicalism drew upon orthodox Protestantism is revealed in a circular letter written by John Wesley in 1764. Hoping to win the support of like-minded Anglican clergy, he described to them what he perceived as the essence of evangelicalism. His ranking order was 'I. Original Sin. II. Justification by Faith. III. Holiness of Heart and Life' (Wesley,

*Journals:* 21, 456). By 'Original sin' Wesley referred to the doctrine that the fall of Adam meant that all human beings were born into an inherited state of sin and that they were therefore so depraved as to be incapable of securing salvation by their own efforts. By 'Justification by Faith' he invoked the Reformation doctrine associated particularly with Martin Luther that justification, that is to say forgiveness of sins through the sacrifice of Christ, could be received only through an intense personal conviction that Christ's atoning death had procured that salvation. By 'Holiness' he meant the spiritual path to be pursued by those who had received justification. Good works and a holy life, however, were of no value if undertaken by those without a personal sense of justification, achieved by faith. Above all, Wesley and other evangelicals strongly repudiated any suggestion that good works could themselves be a sufficient means of attaining salvation; that proposition, they argued, failed to take account of man's fallen and corrupt nature. Salvation could not be achieved by man's own efforts, however morally worthy; it had to come as a divine gift. It will be evident that an emphasis upon sin, and its consequences, together with the hope of redemption offered by the gospel, lay at the heart of the evangelical message.

These principles underpin what remains the most convincing summary of evangelical characteristics by a modern historian. David Bebbington's analysis has, deservedly, been frequently quoted and consists of four vital elements. They are biblicism, crucicentrism, conversionism and activism and they will be discussed in that order (although Dr Bebbington's order is slightly different). Here, priority is given, firstly, to the two elements (biblicism, crucicentrism) which enshrined the beliefs themselves and, secondly, to the two elements (conversionism, activism) which encapsulated the ways in which those beliefs were experienced and communicated.

The Bible stood at the centre of evangelical prayers, preaching and hymns. It was the essential text for theological disputes among themselves and with their non-evangelical critics. Bible study formed the basis of the class-meetings which became so familiar an aspect of Methodism. This was a distillation of the Reformation doctrine that, in the famous words of the seventeenth-century Anglican divine, William Chillingworth, the Bible 'and the Bible only, is the religion of Protestants'. Scripture should be made accessible to all and all had the right and the duty to read it in a search for truth, unimpeded by the mediation of priest and hierarchy. By the end of the eighteenth century, evangelicals were at the forefront of schemes for translating the Bible into vernacular languages. Following the Protestant tradition, they deplored its lack of availability in the vernacular in many Catholic countries. They were united in their conviction that the Bible was the direct result of divine inspiration. Accordingly, it was the ultimate source of authority on all disputed points of doctrine. Of course this was not an evangelical invention; skilled biblical exegesis had long been a vital weapon in theological debates, when the question turned upon, not whether the Bible possessed ultimate authority, but how precisely that authority was to be interpreted. But an important part of the evangelical contribution was, in Chillingworth's phraseology, to stress the word 'only'.

Central to evangelical teaching was the doctrine of the atonement, that the sacrificial death of Christ on the cross was the means by which human sins could be forgiven and man reconciled with God. Hence the cross was the inspiration for innumerable evangelical prayers, sermons and hymns. Again, this was hardly an original doctrine; atonement had been fundamental to Christianity since apostolic times. However, evangelicals tended to take crucicentrism beyond the Catholic position by representing Christ on the cross as suffering himself the death which humanity had deserved through its sinfulness. Their view, following Luther, was that Christ died as a voluntary substitute, paying a debt which he did not owe because humanity had incurred a debt which it could not pay. Christ was depicted as a sacrificial lamb; indeed the lamb became the emblem of the Moravian church and the theme of many of their hymns. Only through the atoning death of Christ could the forgiveness of sins, redemption and ultimate salvation be achieved. Whether Christ's atoning death had redeemed all who were prepared to accept it as an offer of salvation, or whether Christ had died only for a predestined group of the 'chosen', or elect, was to divide evangelicals – at times bitterly – between Arminians (who took the former view) and Calvinists (who held several varieties of the latter view). That division requires separate treatment in chapter four. What is essential for purposes of definition, however, is the way in which 'crucicentrism' was entirely consistent with evangelical notions of man's unworthiness. Only through God's love, manifested in the supreme sacrifice made by Christ on the cross, could fallen man hope for salvation.

How, then, were these teachings to be shared with others? That process had to take place in two stages. The first is described by Dr Bebbington as 'conversionism'. Dr Johnson defined 'conversion' as 'change from reprobation to grace, from a bad to a holy life'. Numerous evangelicals believed that their lives had been completely transformed, sometimes quite suddenly, by a startling experience or series of experiences which subsequently became the defining moments in their lives. Jonathan Edwards generalized from the examples he had encountered in Northampton:

> Persons are first awakened with a sense of their miserable condition by nature and the danger they are in of perishing eternally. Some are more suddenly seized with convictions, by something they hear in public or in private conference; their consciences are suddenly smitten as if their hearts were pierced through with a dart. Others have their awakenings more gradually; they are thoughtful that it is their wisest way to delay no longer ... their awakenings have increased till a sense of their misery has (by the influence of God's Spirit) taken fast hold of them (quoted in Goen (ed.) 1972: 122).

For many, it was a profoundly emotional experience. John Cennick, a future Moravian evangelist in the west of England and in Ireland, described the moment in 1737 in St Lawrence's parish church, Reading, when 'my heart danced for joy and my dying soul revived!' (Cooper 1996: 4). The Lancashire Methodist James Buckley endured bouts of weeping until, on his way to a prayer meeting in 1786, 'I had not walked many yards before I was struck with the greatest amazement: all my darkness instantly turned into light, my grief into joy and despair into a blessed hope full of immortality' (*Arminian Magazine* 1796, 19: 4). In some cases conversion was precipitated by a domestic tragedy or an apparent miracle. The agriculturalist Arthur Young recounted movingly how the death of his fourteen-year-old daughter Martha led him to turn as never before to the New Testament and to evangelical literature, where he found the ability to repent and acquire confidence in immortality. The Methodist James Hall of Manchester, by contrast, found that a cousin's unexpected recovery from illness was 'a means of preparing me to receive the truth' (Betham-Edwards 1898: 282–90; *Arminian Magazine* 1793, **16**: 12). Charles Wesley's hymn offered perhaps the most memorable summary of the sense of release claimed by those who had experienced conversion:

My chains fell off, my heart was free,
I rose, went forth, and followed thee.
(Quoted in Watts 1978: 402)

There was always the danger that the extravagant displays of public emotion which accompanied many conversions would either ebb away, and leave an impression of a highly temporary phenomenon, or would bring evangelicalism into disrepute by their excesses. The latter frequently happened with early Methodism. Edwards and others warned against spurious and doubtful conversions. The way in which conversions were publicized in print, moreover, led others not only to anticipate them but also to deploy predictable and rather stylized language in describing them. Some of the later accounts of conversions in evangelical magazines have a formulaic appearance, as if their authors were merely providing what was expected of them. But although such accounts often have to be studied with scepticism, there is no doubt as to the importance of what they recounted. Conversion led to a 'new birth', a breaking of the will, a resolution, in Zinzendorf's words, 'to stray' from the dear lamb not a quarter of an hour, neither in suggestion nor in fact' (quoted in Ward 1992: 137).

It was the duty of the converted to engage in the fourth major characteristic of evangelicalism, namely 'activism'. The personal experience of the gospel led directly to the obligation to bring its benefit to others. Personal responsibility to God meant that every hour of the day had to be accounted for. The Evangelical Revival was therefore nothing if not energetic and outgoing. Contemporary histories of the subject give a (correct) impression of driven people constantly on the move. To those evangelicals who were already ordained clergy, preaching – if not always at a popular level – was a normal part of their work, but for the relatively ill-educated the prospect of addressing a crowd could be frightening indeed. Numerous memoirs and diaries record moments of terror, prayers for divine guidance and then success. Cennick when preaching for the first time at Kingswood in 1739 was 'afraid lest the Lord should not teach me what to say', but found his prayers answered to the extent that 'many believed in that hour' (Cooper 1996: 6). Early rising, extensive travel and strains upon family life were the norm. The leading figures were indefatigable international travellers; Zinzendorf visited most parts of Europe, the British Isles and North America, Whitefield visited America seven times and died there, while John Wesley covered more than 100,000 miles on his travels. It would perhaps be excessively cynical to refer to 'evangelical tourism', although Harry S. Stout has described Whitefield as 'America's first culture hero' (Stout 1994: 61). However it was largely through evangelical initiative that the immense missionary outpouring of the late eighteenth and nineteenth centuries transformed Protestantism into a world-wide phenomenon. Activism also meant, and required, immediacy. In this respect it echoed the restless impulses of sixteenth-century Puritanism, summed up by the Elizabethan separatist Robert Browne as 'Reformation without tarrying for any' (quoted in Porter 1970: 9), although the reformation intended in the early eighteenth century was of an essentially personal and moral kind. Immediacy also demanded an urgency in bearing witness to the knowledge of one's own justification in order to encourage others to follow the same path.

For all the clarity of Dr Bebbington's definition, evangelicalism was not without apparent contradictions. Three areas where the possibility of contradiction posed a problem deserve mention at this stage. Firstly, evangelicalism carried the most pessimistic assumptions about the dissolute, corrupt nature of fallen man in an age which has been credited with material optimism, confidence in scientific and technological progress, and belief in the human capacity for individual and collective improvement. While new heights of invention and commercial prosperity, at least in Britain, were being achieved, evangelicals emphasized human depravity and helplessness without God's mercy. They made a direct appeal to fear of the punishments of hell, which, to many, including some (like Dr Johnson) among the educated elite, was a terrifying reality. Jonathan Edwards wrote a tract with the title *The Eternity of Hell Torments* and evangelical magazines abounded with tales of the sudden and awful deaths of the unregenerate. Thomas Scott, whose autobiography *The Force of Truth* became a classic, wrote 'I entertained no doubt, but that impenitent sinners would be miserable for ever in hell ... my fears became intolerable' (Scott 1790: 3). Yet at the same time as they gained a reputation (which was not wholly undeserved) for dolefulness and gloomy introversion, evangelicals possessed a vast optimism as to the ultimate triumph of the divine purpose. Every conversion increased that optimism and every report of the success of overseas missions seemed amply to confirm it. Hence they could in some respects find themselves not at odds with the secular spirit of the age but in harmony with it in a perception of human destiny as a broad upward movement towards moral and intellectual betterment.

Secondly, evangelicalism looked backwards, quite consciously, to the Reformation and made a virtue of renewing and re-emphasizing its central doctrines. At the same time its leaders and many of its followers had been educated in an eighteenth-century ethos which included – and in some societies came to be dominated by – scientific revolution and enlightenment. A fundamental and irreconcilable hostility between the European enlightenment and organized religion has long been assumed, no doubt because of the anti-clerical rhetoric of such luminaries as Voltaire. This assumption has been rightly questioned in recent years and affinities between enlightenment and evangelicalism have been delineated (Bebbington 1989: 50–63). It is true that enlightenment thinkers denounced aspects of religious belief as superstitious. David Hume's critique of miracles would be a good example. But other enlightenment characteristics, including the cult of sensibility, the elevation of nature, liberty of conscience and the cultivation of a public morality were far from inconsistent with the moral values of evangelicalism. In a rather engaging phrase, Paul

Johnson characterized Jean-Jacques Rousseau as 'the father of the cold bath, systematic exercise, sport as character-forming, the weekend cottage' (Johnson 1988: 3). Such a characterization might be easily recognized by those who have attended schools where an evangelical ethos prevailed. Nor was it only evangelicals who attacked certain forms of public amusements; Rousseau opposed the opening of a theatre in Geneva, while Diderot severely criticized the lax morality implicit in the works of the 'fête galante' artists.

There were, moreover, assumptions in common. Evangelicals who had experienced persecution were glad to share the enlightenment belief in religious toleration. They strongly upheld the right of private judgement and freedom of the individual conscience. In particular, for all its association with established churches, evangelicalism placed a high value on the voluntary aspects of religion as the divinely inspired movement of the individual human conscience. This in part explains the strong evangelical opposition to the traditional Anglican (and Catholic) doctrine of baptismal regeneration, whereby the Original Sin of the infant at baptism is deemed to be remitted. This is a complex area and John Wesley, for one, was prepared to make allowance for some form of baptismal regeneration. But in general, evangelicals argued that the vital moment comes not with infant baptism (an involuntary act) but with the autonomous exercise of the will at conversion. This concept of the church as a body of willing believers did not contradict enlightenment ideas of voluntary association. Finally, the 'Age of Reason' contributed to the Evangelical Revival the practice in argument and disputation of using reason to justify religious belief. John Wesley constantly referred to 'experimental' religion, meaning the use of the evidence of experience, his own and that of others, to advance his arguments. The elevation of experience over tradition – and sometimes over authority – was a hallmark of evangelicalism.

Thirdly, however, evangelicalism, for all the reliance on reason in the polemic of its leading spokesmen, has been explained at least in part as a reaction against a cold rationality of thought which was fashionable in some intellectual circles in early eighteenth-century Europe. It was at this point that the evangelical insistence upon the supernatural, the miraculous and the providential was particularly apparent. As we have seen, evangelicals viewed religious belief as something highly personal, active, and emotionally sensitive to the divine offer of salvation. The evangelical world was one in which a superintending power could and did intervene providentially in human affairs. When on 15 June 1782 John Wesley emerged virtually unscathed from a fall downstairs in which his 'head rebounded once or twice from the edge of the stone', his comment was 'Doth not God "give his angels charge over us, to keep us in all our ways"?' (Wesley, *Journals*: VI, 243). Henry Venn of Huddersfield assured his children during a thunderstorm that 'the lightning could injure no one, unless with the express permission of that God who directed it' (Venn 1834: 36–7).

There were three specific forms of 'rational' religious thought against which evangelicals reacted strongly. They detested deism, which Wesley defined sharply as 'infidelity, defying the Bible'. Deists accepted a God whose existence was evident in the harmonious nature of the universe but who had stepped back from his own creation and could not be credited with providential interventions which defied the laws of nature. The way in which Deists regarded the Bible as no more than an historical document without divine authority obviously collided with the evangelical insistence on Biblical truth. Similarly, evangelicals had a distaste for Arianism, a fourth-century 'heresy' which denied the true divinity of Christ and accepted the worship of God the Father only. It had some influential eighteenth-century sympathizers in the Church of England and the older Nonconformity. The appeal of the Moravian Church has been partly explained by the way in which it provided an alternative to such heterodoxy. Benjamin La Trobe, a future Moravian minister, seceded from a Dissenting congregation in Dublin because its members were 'half Arians' (Podmore 1994: 171–2).

The strongest evangelical hostility, however, was reserved for Socinianism, a sixteenth-century development of Arianism, which not only denied Christ's divinity but rejected the doctrines of original sin and the atonement. Socinians regarded Christ not as the Son of God but as a man, whose death did not amount to a sacrifice for human sins. Instead, they perceived his death as a splendid example to his followers and as an instance of the way in which society often persecutes enlightened prophets who are ahead of their time. The result was a greatly reduced emphasis upon the horrors of sin and hell, a rejection of the only orthodox (and evangelical) route to salvation and a correspondingly greater confidence in man's ability to save himself. Thomas Scott on reading Socinian literature as a young man found that he 'greedily drank the poison, because it quieted my fears, and flattered my abominable pride' (Scott 1790: 5). The episode helps to carry our definition of evangelicalism a stage further: it was firm in re-emphasizing certain traditional Christian teachings, of which the doctrine of the Trinity was central. Because these forms of 'rational' religion carried much intellectual weight and were argued cogently in print, evangelicals were constantly on the offensive against them. Henry Venn of Huddersfield had what he saw as the 'poison' of Socinianism in mind when he wrote *The Deity of Christ*. Hence one result of the Evangelical Revival was a powerful re-assertion of trinitarianism. It was partly because of the success of the Revival that deism remained a minority affair and had lost much of its impetus by 1750, while Arianism and Socinianism, although remaining important intellectual currents, never acquired popular followings.

An appreciation of earlier developments in the British Isles not only facilitates a general definition of evangelicalism but reinforces our sense of its genuinely eclectic nature. Here the key text, published in 1966, is the study by Dr Walsh. A negative reaction against a rationality which devalued personal, heartfelt religion is indeed one of the formative influences detected by him. However, he also delineates two much more positive influences. These 'taproots' were, firstly, the legacy of the clerical and lay piety of High Church Anglicanism of the late seventeenth and early eighteenth centuries, and, secondly, the survival and at times the recrudescence of some of the Puritan values which in the mid-seventeenth century had enjoyed a temporary political triumph with the overthrow of monarchy and Church (Walsh 1966: 138). Both influences derived directly from ecclesiastical developments in the British Isles in the half century after the Restoration of Charles II in 1660.

From the 1660s, the Church of England, although restored along with the monarchy, was obliged to recognize the existence

of a powerful body of Protestant opinion which did not accept its authority. Indeed, there was enacted a battery of legislation designed to repress that opinion, to which the term 'Dissent' or 'Nonconformity' began to be applied. At the parish level, many Anglican clergy understood that the allegiance of their parishioners would have to be won – and retained – in a period of genuine competition from these successors of the mid-century Puritans. There followed a flowering of voluntary activity, spearheaded by the Anglican clergy, since the Church 'because it could not effectively coerce, had to persuade' (Walsh 1986: 279). This activity was greatly stimulated – from necessity – by the Revolution of 1688–9. The accession of William III and Mary led to a fundamental change of ecclesiastical régime. The Toleration Act of 1689 allowed Protestant Dissenters, so long as they were trinitarian and registered their meeting-houses, to worship legally. Immediately, many hundreds of Presbyterian, Independent, Baptist and, to a lesser extent, Quaker places of worship appeared and in some areas flourished. At the same time, the Church of England's Scottish cousin, the Episcopalian Church, was disestablished and its bitter rival, the Presbyterian Church, became (and remains) the established church north of the border.

The attendant Anglican insecurity and nervousness produced a number of national societies on a voluntary basis which had the objective of seeking to restore and enhance respect for Anglican theological and social values. Three of them are particularly relevant to evangelicalism. The Society for Promoting Christian Knowledge (SPCK) was founded in 1698 by the Rector of Sheldon (Warwickshire) Thomas Bray. Its objectives included the publication and popularization of Bibles and other religious literature and the construction of charity schools in as many parts of the country as possible. It met with particular success in Wales, and the promotion of popular Anglican literature and instruction in Welsh helps to explain some of the early support for the Welsh evangelists of the 1720s and 1730s – as well as why the great Welsh revival took place largely under Anglican leadership. Bray was also a founder of the Society for the Propagation of the Gospel in Foreign Parts (SPG) in 1701 which raised funds for missionary work, mainly in North America and the Caribbean. Bray himself went to Maryland and it was under the auspices of the SPG that the Wesley brothers made their dramatic, if not startlingly successful, expedition to Georgia in 1735. In addition, a series of societies for the reformation of manners emerged, to regulate public morality by exhortation and, where necessary, by prosecution. Their targets were mainly the types of vice, such as lewdness and profanity, traditionally associated with the lower orders. But in seeking to enforce observation of the sabbath, in censuring the theatre in the age of Congreve and Vanbrugh and – a little later – in campaigning against the availability of cheap gin, these societies obviously prefigured much of what Wilberforce and his associates sought to achieve at the end of the eighteenth century.

These were national, if primarily metropolitan, societies. At local level, too, Anglican voluntary activity went far beyond the formal round of regular church services. Encouraged initially in the 1670s by Anthony Horneck, Vicar of All Saints, Oxford, and by birth a German Protestant and former student at Heidelberg, these religious societies offered weekly gatherings for spiritual conversation. They pursued 'real holiness of heart and life' with meetings small enough to permit frank self-examination and mutual support, while basing their approach upon the Bible and the Book of Common Prayer. They were exclusively Anglican, of most appeal to respectable tradesmen and – presumably – entirely male in membership. Horneck himself had become a celebrated preacher by the 1680s and he and his friend William Smythies, a London clergyman, had helped to establish over 40 societies, or clubs, of this sort in the capital alone by 1700 (Walsh 1986: 281; Spurr 1993: 132–3). A modest pamphlet describing their growth, *An Account of the Rise and Progress of the Religious Societies in London*, published by the clergyman Josiah Woodward in 1699, became not only a standard history but a blueprint for the foundation of further societies.

Although it has been suggested that these religious societies had lost much of their impetus by the late 1730s, they had set a precedent of voluntary activity which was of considerable value to the evangelicals of that decade. They also reflected a degree of High Church piety which represented the most traditional of Anglican values – a claim to apostolic succession in the priesthood, the importance of baptismal regeneration, the centrality of the Sacrament and the regulation of worship and rites of passage according to the Book of Common Prayer. It was quite consistent for High Churchmen to uphold the Church's institutional authority on the one hand and to promote personal religious and moral reformation on the other. Their contribution to this cause was considerable. So, too, was that of the non-jurors, who had left the Church in the early 1690s when their consciences would not permit them to take the oaths of loyalty to the régime of William III. A subsequent exponent of that tradition, William Law (1686–1761), wrote a formidable and widely read tract entitled *A Serious Call to a Devout and Holy Life* (1728), which enjoined a personal regime of total religious devotion coupled with extreme asceticism and withdrawal from the world. Wesley, Whitefield and Henry Venn all studied it carefully; Samuel Johnson was almost driven to a nervous breakdown by his failure to live up to its impossibly demanding precepts. A significant number of Evangelicals came from High Church backgrounds, while many of their successors in the early nineteenth century, including members of the Wilberforce family, returned to a High Church affinity.

Alongside the High Church ancestry of English and Welsh evangelicalism, Dr Walsh has placed the spiritual legacy of seventeenth-century Puritanism. The successors to the Puritans of the Interregnum period, far from being Regicides, were for the most part moderate Presbyterians who accepted the idea of a single national church, albeit one with significant reforms to accommodate their own preferences. Failure to engineer compromise between them and the restored Anglican authorities resulted in the departure from the Church of some 2,000 clergy with Puritan sympathies between 1660 and 1662. Thereafter, their existence, at first illegal and (after 1689) acknowledged by the state, came to be seen as the formal, institutional beginning of separate English and Welsh Nonconformity. As they gradually acquired wealth and social respectability, they moved further away from their radical forebears of the 1650s. But the Puritan ethos remained. It gave the individual's personal relationship with God a far higher priority than respect for the ecclesiastical hierarchy, inculcated the kind of self-analysis which often found expression in spiritual autobiographies, encouraged the involvement of lay (including female) preaching and bore the sort of democratic implications which were evident among the German Pietists. The presence of these characteristics in the early stages of the Evangelical Revival helps to explain why Dr Johnson defined Methodists in 1755 as 'A new sect of Puritans lately arisen'. The more extreme Puritans of the seventeenth century, such as the Fifth Monarchy Men in England and the Cameronians in Scotland, were defeated militarily, but one might still ask what became of the more moderate eirenical Puritan ethos. The answer is that in terms of spirituality it continued, expressed in such works as Richard Baxter's *Call to the Unconverted* and in the pastoral work of often obscure Dissenting ministers. Two examples in the mountainous region of Derbyshire suggest early intimations of evangelical itinerancy. William Bagshawe (1628–702) was one of the ejected of 1662 who preached regularly in small Derbyshire villages at some personal risk and became known as the 'Apostle of the Peak'. A generation later the Dissenter James Clegg (1679–1755) of Chapel en le Frith travelled extensively in the same scattered community while preaching and, in his medical capacity, treating fevers, tuberculosis and quinsies. The practice of the itinerant preacher was much more a Puritan – and indeed earlier – legacy than a Methodist invention.

These definitions of, and problems concerning, evangelicalism have focused primarily upon the British Isles. This has been deliberate. Although a conscious search for 'pre-conditions' may well incur the charge of taking advantage of hindsight, enough has perhaps been said to show that the famous events of the 1730s were neither inexplicable nor miraculous. They had firm historical causes and precedents and most of those causes and precedents may be found within the contemporary Church of England.

# CHAPTER THREE

# Revival and the existing British churches

In the British Isles during the 1730s and 1740s there took place a series of separate and independent religious revivals, each of which appears to have begun spontaneously. It is true that they had characteristics in common and that such characteristics make it possible for these revivals to be considered under one heading, 'Revival', which may be dignified with a capital 'R'. Some of those characteristics were discussed in the previous chapter. But the primary causes of each revival were local and specific. These separate revivals were transformed from local to national, and then to international, phenomena by the way in which they took place within the same brief period of time, and by the way in which each quickly became known and aroused outside interest. Developments among the German Pietists do not fully explain what happened among the early Welsh evangelicals or in a small parish in rural Lanarkshire. But they do make it easier to understand why and how revivalists in one part of a country, continent or hemisphere rapidly acquired information about new revivals elsewhere and in many cases set out to join, stimulate and prolong them. The apparent spontaneity of the revivals, with no apparent single organizing agency or a single material explanation, led evangelicals themselves to interpret what was happening in terms of the divine will, an outpouring of the Holy Spirit.

Another traditional explanation of the revivals has been based upon perceived inadequacies of existing churches. The limitations of the orthodox Lutheran Church in Saxony and Brandenburg-Prussia, as we have seen, have been held up as leaving a spiritual and in some senses material vacuum to be filled by Francke and his associates. Can the early stages of the revival in the British Isles be attributed to some kind of doctrinal, pastoral or charitable failure on the part of the Church of England? In part, perhaps, it can. Clearly, however, Anglican failure will hardly serve as a satisfactory international explanation for revival. But since the Anglican Church exercised such influence in England, Wales, Ireland and the colonies, its general character was of crucial importance to some of the focal points of evangelicalism. The Church was integral to the constitution and to society. As the Scottish novelist and well-travelled ship's doctor Tobias Smollett wrote to an English friend in 1758 'I consider the Church not as a religious but as a political Establishment so minutely interwoven in our Constitution that the one cannot be detached from the other, without the most imminent danger of Destruction to both' (quoted in Knapp (ed.), 1970: 73).

Contemporary and subsequent criticisms of the early eighteenth-century Church of England have tended to focus upon three main areas. The first is an alleged political subservience on the part of the Church to an increasingly secularized state, dominated from 1714 by a series of Whig ministries. The Church, according to this critique, became little more than an agency of the Whig state, with its main priority the preaching of civic order rather than the saving of souls. In return, the state protected the Church's privileges, which included a virtual monopoly of public life as the Test and Corporation Acts excluded non-Anglicans from national and local office. William Warburton in his *Alliance between Church and State* (1736) accepted that the Church should end any pretensions to independence from the state in return for such protection. His tract has been construed as a representative statement of clerical opinion. The loss of independence was evident in the Whig government's effective suppression of Convocation, the 'Parliament' of the Anglican clergy, from 1717, lest it give the Church's (Tory) critics of the ministry a platform for opposition. Similarly, the Whigs tried unsuccessfully in 1719 and in the late 1740s to regulate the University of Oxford in their own interests, a matter of some importance given Oxford's strongly Tory complexion and the part which the University played in the Evangelical Revival. Whigs were appointed to the most senior positions in the Church – one of the most extreme cases being that of Benjamin Hoadly, who became Bishop of the poverty-stricken diocese of Bangor in 1715 but (uniquely in the eighteenth century) received three further translations thereafter, ending his career as Bishop of Winchester. Some of the Whig appointees seemed to reflect an indifference to traditional doctrine; the nomination of Thomas Rundle to the bishopric of Gloucester in 1734 provoked an outcry because of his unorthodox opinions. The dominant mentality of the age has been summed up as 'erastian' (signifying the subordination of the Church to the state) and 'latitudinarian' (signifying, not altogether fairly, a tolerance born of indifference to doctrine). As a result, the main obsession of the clergy was the pursuit of patronage and outright careerism. There is, perhaps, a refreshing lack of cant and posturing in the letter from the Rev. Henry Gally, prebend of Norwich, to the Duke of Newcastle in 1766: 'The Dean of Wells is dead. I hope yr Grace will think of me to succeed him' (B.L. Add. MS 32973, f. 170).

Yet this was very far from the whole story. It is questionable as to whether Warburton really spoke for the majority of the Anglican clergy; in 1741 he was turned down for an Oxford Doctor of Divinity. Many clergy retained their Tory convictions at the expense of their careers. The religious nature of the Tory mentality is illustrated in John Wesley's definition of a Tory as 'one who believes God, not the people, to be the origin of all civil power' (quoted in Clark 1985: 237). It was because the bulk of the lower clergy remained obstinately Tory that the Whig ministries found it necessary to suspend Convocation. Although some clergy undoubtedly embraced Whiggism to advance their careers, most did not. In Cheshire, for instance, the evidence of poll books reveals that a majority of clergymen who voted continued to support Tory candidates in general elections until mid-century, although in a system of open voting such behaviour was known, recorded and could have damaging consequences for the voter (Baskerville 1987: 79–81). An interpretation of the early stages of the Evangelical Revival as, at least in part, a Tory revolt against cynical Whig control of the Church would be incomplete but far from wholly inaccurate.

Yet the political nature of the Whig regime itself was not necessarily inconsistent with respect for the traditions and privileges of the Church. The successive Whig ministries between 1714 and 1760 did not amount to an unchanging unity. Gradually, successive Whig ministers became more sensitive to clerical concerns. Lord Stanhope, the leading Whig minister between 1714 and 1721 was, admittedly, very sympathetic towards Dissenters and would have gladly deprived the Church of its monopoly of public office by repealing the Test laws; but his successor, Sir Robert Walpole, although not a convinced religious believer, recognized the value of the Church as a social institution and resisted pressures for such repeal. The Duke of Newcastle, whose ascendancy in Church affairs lasted from the late 1730s to the 1760s, was a devout Anglican who held regular family prayers. He took very seriously the doctrinal orthodoxy of candidates for the episcopate. By mid-century, many parochial clergy, including some from traditional Tory backgrounds, found it less and less distasteful to support Whig parliamentary candidates. There were, moreover, 'Church Whigs', who combined Whig principles, notably support for the Hanoverian succession and toleration for Dissenters, with a strong insistence on the Church's special role in society. Of these, the most outstanding individual was Edmund Gibson (1669–1748) Bishop of London. Though a strong critic of Methodism, which he regarded as a form of deluded emotionalism, Gibson was a powerful defender of the Church's interests. In 1736 he sacrificed his political relationship with Walpole when he and a majority of his fellow bishops used their positions in the House of Lords to defeat a ministerial attempt to weaken the system of tithe payment. It was partly because of pressure from 'Church Whigs' that the unorthodox Rundle did not obtain an English bishopric and had to be content with one in Ireland.

The second charge traditionally levelled against the Georgian Church is that of pastoral neglect. It was common form amongst nineteenth-century radicals, reformers and many historians to dismiss the eighteenth-century Church as self-interested, materialistic and indifferent to the spiritual needs of the people. Charges of this nature reached a height of vehemence in 1820, when the Unitarian John Wade published *The Black Book; or Corruption Unmasked*, a work several times republished and updated. Wade depicted a Church with vast inequalities of income between senior clergy and their juniors, who served as curates in poor parishes with remuneration at little more than starvation level. The result had been pluralism, non-residence, and a spiritual vacuum which was supposedly waiting for the Evangelical Revival to fill it. Writing of the primacy of Archbishop Wake of Canterbury in the mid-1730s, two nineteenth-century clerical historians with impeccable credentials complained 'The sleepy time had set in so far as practical activity was concerned' (Overton & Relton 1906: 28). The impression of somnolence is reinforced by Dr Johnson's definition of the word 'revival' itself as 'recall from a state of languor, oblivion or obscurity'.

Such allegations against church establishments have been made in many societies since time immemorial and the eighteenth century has been the victim of the following century's self-congratulatory sense of progression from a low base. Many of the more extreme allegations of *The Black Book* were grossly exaggerated and politically motivated. Since the work of Norman Sykes began to appear in the 1930s, there has been a cautiously optimistic re-assessment of the work of the Georgian clergy. That non-residence existed, of course, cannot be denied, and at times it reached a substantial scale. In the county of Devon in 1744 there were 114 non-resident clergy out of a total of 332; in 1764 the figure was 147 of 372 and in 1779 it was 159 of 390 (Warne 1969: 38–9). In east Yorkshire in mid-century, only 21 of 78 vicarages surveyed had a resident clergyman, while 60 of 95 curacies had a non-resident to perform church services (Evans 1987: 233). But this was not nationally typical. The Church contained many regional variations and it tended to be in upland areas with large parishes and scattered populations that the pastoral work of the clergy was placed under most strain. At the same time, however, it was in the upland parishes of the north where some of the most dedicated parish clergy, such as William Grimshaw of Haworth, were to be found. Non-residence was not necessarily more prevalent in the north than in the south (Mather 1985: 268) and in both regions it could often be explained by the low stipends which made it necessary for a clergyman to hold more than one living in order to secure a tolerable income.

The reasons for such low stipends and the extent of pluralism have been explained in contradictory ways. The most familiar explanation cites an overpopulated clerical profession in which too many university graduates were scrambling for too few livings. A more original explanation, however, suggests that a declining number of candidates for the profession meant that many livings were left unfilled (Virgin 1989: 136). Non-residence, in any case, did not necessarily imply an absence of church services; an impression survives of a hard-worked clergy labouring diligently to provide services in unfamiliar and difficult conditions, one of which was competition from Dissent. Dr Gregory's study of the diocese of Canterbury reveals a generally conscientious parish clergy which, while at times requiring prodding from above, attended to its regular duties of conducting services, baptizing, catechizing children and providing as many services as the laity required and as the ecclesiastical conventions of the age demanded (Gregory 1993: 79–85). Although 'there is some evidence of a secular fall in the number of Sunday services during the eighteenth century' there was also considerable variation and in many areas there was monthly communion, as distinct from the quarterly celebration which has often been regarded as the eighteenth-century norm (Mather 1985: 269–72). The pattern of Methodist success and relative failure is partly accounted for by the highly variegated pattern of religious provision offered by the established church.

Other recent research has revealed a much deeper level of support at local level for the Church than has always been appreciated. In Oldham and Saddleworth the Church retained a considerable loyalty throughout the eighteenth century by church-building, frequent preaching and home visits (Smith 1994: ch. vii). An effective and committed lay patron could make all the difference. The rector of East Hendred, Berkshire, George Woodward, was almost lyrical in praise of his lay benefactor, Mr Wymondesold:

His parish will feel his absence, for he does a great deal of good amongst them, and employs a great many poor people: he has this and the last summer been about a very good piece of work; he has undertaken the repair and beautifying of his parish church ... and he has made it from a little, dark, indecent place, one of the prettiest, neatest churches that we have any where at all; the pews have all been new built in a more commodious manner, the reading desk, clerk's seat,

and pulpit, all enlarged and new painted, the chancel well
repaired, and the Commandments, Lord's Prayer, and Belief,
new done, and properly placed (Gibson, D. (ed.) 1982: 93).

Evidence of loyalty to the Church outside the elite, moreover, is
provided by the popular journalism of the strident Anglican
Nathaniel Mist's *Weekly Journal: or Saturday's Post* and, more
violently, by the incidence of sporadic rioting against Dissenters
and (especially in the 1740s) against Methodists. There was also a
substantial lay market for the literature of Anglican devotion. The
Restoration classic *The Whole Duty of Man* was never out of
print during the eighteenth century, and when the Evangelical
minister Henry Venn published *The Complete Duty of Man* in
1763 it quickly went through twenty editions.

The third form of contemporary criticism of the Church concerned its alleged promotion of morality at the expense of the
need for repentance, justification and salvation from sin. The
thirty-nine Articles of the Church of England, formulated after
much wrangling early in the reign of Queen Elizabeth, amounted
to a repository of Protestant doctrine. Specific articles affirmed
doctrines which enshrined some of the evangelical ideas examined
in chapter two. Article 11 proclaimed justification by faith alone;
article 12 asserted that good works, though to be valued as evidence of faith, cannot atone for sins. Article 13 denounced works
done before the receipt of justification as 'not pleasant to God',
while article 17 was a statement of the moderate Calvinist position of predestination. The evangelicals did not introduce novel
doctrines; they insisted on the revitalization of existing doctrines
and adopted new methods of proclaiming them. The emphasis on
morality and the 'reasonable' and intellectually polished manner
in which it was preached was widely attributed to the first Archbishop of Canterbury of the post-Revolution period, John Tillotson (1630–94), whose style of preaching served as an exemplar for
generations of clergymen. To many evangelicals, however, such
an approach seemed to be a retreat from the Reformation doctrines contained in the articles, an unnecessary concession to an
age of reason and scientific discovery and a dangerous reversion to
the allegedly 'popish' belief that salvation could be procured by
good works and morally appropriate conduct.

Their anxieties were encapsulated by one of the earliest members of the Holy Club in Oxford, John Gambold. The Reformation doctrines of redemption and free grace, he wrote, had caused such fear in the rebellious 1640s that:

> The Divines of the Establishment turned the scale as much as they could the other way, putting the Gospel as much as they could in a moral & rational light till by degrees & by following that Taste ... it has been of late boldly suggested that there is or ought to be nothing in the Gospel any farther than Natural Religion (quoted in Boynton 1994: 308).

Perhaps one should point out, however, that the traits of which Gambold complained were neither completely devoid of religious conviction based on the Bible nor were they universally shared within the Church. Gambold was referring principally to the senior clergy who owed their preferments to the post-1688 regime. But the Revival itself shows how far the Reformation doctrines still carried allegiance within the Church, both among clergy and laity. It cannot be emphasized too strongly that forms of belief and devotion which would later be called Evangelical were to be found in the Church well before the famous conversion of John Wesley in 1738. It was not the case that Methodism, springing up *ex nihilo*, revitalized a dormant church. It would be more accurate to say that a series of Gospel-minded and often moderate Calvinist elements within the Church stimulated the Evangelical Revival, of which Methodism was one, and only one, component. The pattern for the early evangelicals tended to be one where they experienced conversion and only then actually encountered a prominent Methodist such as Wesley or Whitefield, rather than vice versa.

This immediately becomes clear if one examines the careers of the leading Anglican clergy associated with the revival. It is appropriate to begin with a consideration of the 'Holy Club' at Oxford, since it drew together so many international strands. Although the claim that it was founded by the Wesley brothers in 1729 is still widely accepted, it is also recognized that there existed within the different Oxford colleges several such clubs which, to some extent, drew on the example of the religious societies of the Horneck and Woodward type (Rack 1989: 87). Their practices, too, included weekly (and subsequently more frequent) meetings for Bible study and spiritual self-examination, personal asceticism, a sense of accountability to God which often led to auto-biographical writing and journal-keeping and charitable work, which in Oxford is best remembered for prison visits to the condemned (Walsh 1986: 286). Its continuity with post-1660 Anglican practice was apparent, as was the sense of dissatisfaction, expressed by Gambold, with the tone of much of the clerical (and governmental) hierarchy. Its members included the Manchester clergyman and Jacobite sympathizer John Clayton, together with the future Moravian Benjamin Ingham, and the future parish priests Christopher Atkinson, Charles Kinchin and John White-lamb. As a group they were somewhat diverse; those, like the Wesley brothers and Whitefield, who became pioneers of Methodism, will feature prominently in the next chapter. So will those who became Moravians. The Holy Club, however, and Oxford University more generally were far from the only sources of Revival within the Church.

A series of independent conversions among the clergy in different parts of the country occurred in the 1720s and 1730s. George Thomson of St Gennys in Cornwall was one of them; James Hervey, curate of Bideford in Devon, was another. Vincent Perronet of Shoreham was ten years older than John Wesley, converted independently of him and did not meet him for the first time until 1744. William Romaine (1714–95), though an undergraduate at Wesley's former Oxford college, did not associate with the Holy Club and only converted subsequently; later he became a vital inspiration for the revival in London. Henry Venn (1725–97), an able cricketer at Cambridge University, turned towards Evangelical values shortly afterwards while serving as a curate in Surrey. His son explained his conversion:

This change of his sentiments was not to be ascribed to an intercourse with others: it was the steady progress of his mind, in consequence of a faithful and diligent application to the Holy Scriptures ... it was not till some years afterwards that he became acquainted with any of those preachers who are usually known by the name of Evangelical (Venn 1834: 22).

Venn became father to an important clerical dynasty which carried Evangelicalism (via his son) to the famous Clapham sect and (via his curate at Huddersfield, John Riland) to Warwickshire.

There is no single explanation for these and other contemporaneous conversions. Perronet, Romaine, Charles Edward de Coetlogon and several others came from Huguenot backgrounds, which re-emphasizes the international context of the conversion experience. The legacy of the religious societies cannot be discounted, nor can the patronage of a small number of the aristocratic elite. The relative independence conferred by wealth and status, moreover, opened the door to female piety. The conventions of eighteenth-century society permitted, and at times encouraged, the endowment by a spinster, a widow, even at times a married woman, of a genuinely pious cause. The early stages of the Revival benefited from the sponsorship of several ladies of the nobility. They included Lady Gertrude Hotham, sister of the celebrated fourth Earl of Chesterfield, whose *Letters to his Son* embodied precepts of a markedly non-evangelical kind. Lady Arabella Denny founded the Magdalene Chapel in Dublin in 1773 and helped to make it a centre for evangelical preachers (Hempton and Hill 1992: 131).

However, the most important of these blue-blooded patrons was Selina, Countess of Huntingdon (1701–91), an aristocrat both by birth and marriage who was converted to a Calvinist form of Evangelicalism in the late 1730s. The example of her husband's half-sister, Lady Betty Hastings, and her own charitable work were the main influences which led her in that direction. She had strong support from her family and her latest biographer refutes the myth that her husband opposed her conversion (Welch 1995: 43). It is true that her family came to know the Yorkshire Evangelist Benjamin Ingham very well – indeed, he married her sister-in-law – and that they turned to the Moravians for comfort at a time of bereavement. Once again, however, it was a case of conversion leading to, rather than following, contact with other Evangelicals. The significance of the Countess's involvement lay in the wealth and ecclesiastical patronage which her family possessed. She used her Leicestershire estates at Donnington Park as a base for Evangelical activity, providing books for the religious society formed by the Rev. Edward Ellis nearby and inviting him to preach at the Park. By encouraging her servant David Taylor to form new societies in the county, she anticipated the kind of problem which would quickly beset the revival: that of the unlettered layman who appeared to challenge the authority of the local Anglican clergy (Welch 1995: 48–9). But she also provided practical help for Evangelical clergymen by making them her chaplains and using her London houses to give them access to a metropolitan audience. It was her patronage of George Whitefield which so strengthened the Calvinist branch of the Revival, even after her followers were forced out of the Church of England in the 1780s. In 1761 she financed a chapel at Brighton, and subsequently others in Bath, Tunbridge Wells, Dublin and Swansea. She leased buildings for religious purposes in less fashionable areas, such as Wapping, and provided a minister for an existing Dissenting congregation at Shoreditch. The Moorfields Tabernacle, where Whitefield preached, became an important centre for her followers in London.

These conversions, all within the Church of England itself, together with the work of influential members of the lay elite, reveal a repository of spiritual potential which seriously challenges the more familiar image of a dominant Anglican latitudinarianism. The same is true of the state of the Church of England in Wales. The assumptions that the Welsh revival was a reaction against the torpor and abuses of the Anglican Church in the principality, and that the arrival of the invigorating force of Methodism was a decisive break with the past, have been effectively demolished by the research of such scholars as Geraint H. Jenkins. The preaching of the Anglican clergy in Wales, can hardly be indicted for excessive and abstruse rationality, and one popular preacher in particular, the Rev. Griffith Jones, Rector of Llanddowror in Carmarthenshire, incurred between 1714 and 1718 many of the criticisms which were hurled at John Wesley nearly thirty years later – breaches of church order and 'invading' the parishes of his fellow-clergy. Jones's audiences have been estimated in their thousands (Jenkins 1978: 14–15). According to one (admittedly sympathetic) source, the circulating schools which Jones ran taught the astonishingly high number of 150,212 people to read the Welsh Bible (Young 1893: 28). There was certainly a large increase in the quantity of religious literature produced in the Welsh language; it included almanacs and ballads as well as Bibles and devotional tracts. This was partly the result of the efforts of the voluntary Anglican societies of the early eighteenth century, notably the SPCK and the charity schools. Even when allowance is made for the fact that approximately half of these books and pamphlets were translations from the original English, and that the SPCK was rather inclined to regard the Welsh language with condescension, it is clear that there was both a demand for, and supply of, the spoken and written word and that Anglican spirituality was far from extinct. Without the religious and educational developments in Wales during the half-century before the advent of Methodism there could hardly have been that Welsh revival which – crucially – preceded that in England (Jenkins 1978: 34–8, 305–9).

The earliest stages of the Welsh revival also remind us of the vital contribution of the Anglican laity. Howel Harris (1714–73) of Breconshire, whose conversion in 1735 was accompanied by what became the familiar evangelical sense of overwhelming sin, was repeatedly refused Anglican ordination because of the irregularity of his preaching. From 1737 Harris and his co-worker Daniel Rowland, curate of Llangeitho in Cardiganshire, developed the kind of itinerant preaching and the groups of small religious societies which soon characterized the revival as a whole. For all their subsequent quarrels, Harris and Rowland were pioneers not only in the Welsh, but in the overall British, sense. Their methods became more widely known partly because there was a Welsh Anglican presence in Oxford University. Jesus College was a Welsh foundation, while Harris studied briefly at St Mary Hall in 1735. The Welsh revival sprang from the Church of England and was an indigenous Welsh phenomenon. It derived from a popular Anglicanism within the principality, not a campaign of proselytizing by English 'missionaries'.

The Church of England was also the established church in Ireland. Here, however, the Revival took a very different form. The Earl of Tyrconnel, as Lord Lieutenant, and many members of the Irish Parliament had remained loyal to James II in 1688–9. Much of the Catholic majority had rebelled against the imposition of the Protestant regime of William and Mary. It subsequently remained at best sullenly acquiescent in the rule of a Protestant Lord Lieutenant, a Dublin Parliament which was exclusively Protestant (and, by the Declaratory Act of 1719, subordinate to the Parliament at Westminster) and a body of landowners many of whom looked to England as their home. Although there was certainly a modest economic improvement in the eighteenth century, and the Jacobites made little impact in Ireland, the bulk of the population remained solid in its Catholic allegiance and was hardly likely to respond warmly to a movement which had some of its roots in a vehement anti-Catholicism. The Church of Ireland, however, despite its established status, its four archbishops and eighteen bishops, was not the chosen faith even of a majority of the Protestant population. The Presbyterians, who were mainly, of course, Scottish in origin were firmly Dissenting in ethos, unlike the Presbyterian Church in Scotland itself, which enjoyed established status.

It is noteworthy that in Ireland – even in Dublin, where the revival made its initial impact – many of what with hindsight might be termed the pre-conditions of revival in England and Wales were absent. Indigenous religious societies, for instance, had made little impression. The early revivalists were English evangelists, notably John Cennick, who began his preaching mission in Dublin in June 1746. Wesley first visited the city the following year. Yet there were two elements in Irish society which provided raw material for their endeavours. Firstly there were small colonies of Protestant refugees from the Palatinate of the Rhine, who had fled the French armies during the War of Spanish Succession (1702–13); they provided some early Methodist recruits. Secondly, there had developed among some of the Ulster Presbyterians the same rationalizing tendency as that detectable in the intellectual climate of England. In the 1720s a breakaway group in Antrim rejected much of the orthodox, reformed Calvinist teaching of their Presbyterian co-religionists and evolved a separate existence as the 'non-subscribing Presbyterians'. In theology they became increasingly non-trinitarian in the Arian sense discussed briefly in chapter two. In so doing, they gave the evangelicals an opportunity to reassert their own conceptions of traditional Christian doctrines, of which, as we have seen, trinitarianism was one. In Ireland, however, the most notable preachers were English and, to a lesser extent, Welsh. Some of the best Irish Evangelical preachers, such as William Tennent and his sons, made their names in America.

The writ of the Church of England, however, did not run in Scotland. The success of the Covenanters against the Episcopalian, or Anglican, rule of Charles I in the mid-seventeenth century had been crowned in 1689-90 when the regime of William and Mary recognized the strongly Presbyterian Church, or Kirk, as the established church. This left the Scottish Episcopalians, who were thus deprived of the privileges of establishment, as a declining, aggrieved minority with inclinations towards Jacobitism. Association with the state, however, led some members of the Kirk to fear that secular interests were corrupting its original Calvinist purity, and there were small secessions in the eighteenth century, notably that of Ebenezer Erskine and his 'Associate presbytery' in 1733. The Kirk attempted to bring the reformed religion to the Highlands, building on older Covenanting traditions and adding some of the methods of the German Pietists, such as prayer meetings with an active lay involvement. Although handicapped by the inaccessibility of the English language to a population with a Gaelic tongue which lacked the print culture of Welsh, these efforts produced a long-term, if unspectacular, revival in the Highlands. But the established clergy of the Kirk had little time for the kind of popular religion which involved irregularities of preaching (mainly outdoors) and eccentricities of personal behaviour (mainly convulsions) at religious worship.

There was none the less within Scottish Presbyterianism a revival tradition with seventeenth-century antecedents. There had been revivals at Stewarton and Irvine in 1625 and at Kirk of Shotts five years later. It was a combination of traditions of this sort and accounts of Jonathan Edwards and the 'awakening' in Massachusetts which seems to have created an atmosphere of religious expectancy in parts of lowland Scotland during the early 1740s. If a completely unpredictable revival could take place in a relatively remote part of New England, why not in a country where Protestantism was not only established but had popular roots? A heritage from the spirit of religious independence and individual conscience proclaimed by the Covenanting spirit had been a growing interest in, and demand for, prayer societies which met at private houses for regular Bible study and spiritual self-examination. They pre-dated both the New England revival and the advent of Methodism. Although they owed their origins to Scottish impulses, they bore at least some resemblance to the societies of Halle and to the pre-1740 religious societies in England. Ebenezer Erskine had founded one at Portmoak as early as 1714. It was through such societies that news of international religious developments was communicated and the hope of a Scottish revival stimulated. That hope blossomed briefly but in a spectacular way at Cambuslang in Lanarkshire in the early months of 1742. The minister of the parish, William McCulloch, was well aware of the success of Edwards and Whitefield and through his *Glasgow Weekly History* he publicized the New England revival while at the same time reading to his own congregation letters from correspondents with direct experience of revivals elsewhere. He was asked by a group of his parishioners to give a weekly lecture on a weekday evening and quickly found himself preaching to 20,000–30,000 people. Since the population of Cambuslang was smaller than one thousand, the extent of his popular appeal is obvious. Though not an itinerant, McCulloch bears comparison with Whitefield, who had preached in Glasgow and Edinburgh shortly beforehand and soon visited McCulloch's own parish. McCulloch gained several hundred converts and – very helpfully – recorded the spiritual experiences of 110 of them (Fawcett 1971: 5–7). His record shows that this group were drawn mainly from small tenants and craftsmen, servants and the unskilled; it included a high number of unmarried women (Smout 1982: 116–7). The low social status of those involved was probably an implicit protest against the oligarchic nature of the Kirk and the propertied elite which dominated parish life through lay patronage of ministerial appointments. The Cambuslang revival was frowned upon by the Kirk's rulers and, partly for that reason it – and a similar revival at Kilsyth – did not give birth to a wider movement. As Professor Ward puts it 'Like the revival in New England to which it was so closely linked, the revival in the Lowlands bloomed only for a day' (Ward 1992: 339).

What happened subsequently to McCulloch's converts and hearers? Although millennial expectations of an evangelical conversion of the whole of Scotland were disappointed, the revival spread. Other religious societies appeared, such as those of Thomas Gillespie at Carnock and Dunfermline, while at Cambuslang itself the church kept a day of fasting and thanksgiving on the anniversary of the events of 1742 (Roxburgh 1994: 271–2). The lessons for the historian are fourfold. Firstly, the international dimension was particularly apparent at Cambuslang, but secondly, without such indigenous factors as the strongly Protestant sentiment in the Lowlands and memories of bitter conflicts over ministerial appointments, that international dimension could hardly have made such an impact. Thirdly, the Church of Scotland, like its English counterpart, possessed a potentially evangelical element long before the conventionally-understood beginning of the Revival. Fourthly, the high levels of literacy displayed by McCulloch's converts, despite their humble social status, underline the extent to which an existing print culture was an essential condition for the Revival's success.

So far, this chapter has considered the state of the established churches in the British Isles at the beginning of the Evangelical Revival. It concludes with a brief examination of the English Dissenting denominations. If the stereotype of the Church of England as moribund has been fundamentally revised, that process has not been applied so thoroughly to the post-1660 Protestant Dissenters. The English Presbyterians, the largest of their denominations, have been particularly stigmatized as increasingly arid and intellectually abstruse in their theology, alienating their flocks with Arian notions of the Trinity and obsessed with internal conflict. It has been suggested that Nonconformity tended towards either Arianism or High Calvinism. The former looked askance upon original sin and the compelling need for repentance; the latter was hardly consistent with 'activism' and preaching to the unconverted because of its belief in predestination. It is certainly true that disputes over the Trinity were frequent within Old Dissent, especially among Presbyterians and General Baptists, and that there is evidence of a decline in Dissenting numbers in the early eighteenth century.

Although such a decline was perceived and commented upon by Dissenters themselves, it does not follow that it resulted from theological speculation or a retreat from the Calvinist zeal of the Commonwealth and Restoration periods. An equally plausible explanation is the economic decline of the trades and industries which had previously supported Dissenting congregations, particularly in Wiltshire and Hampshire. As an anonymous Dissenting commentator put it in 1731, 'The strength of our interest lies amongst the middling and trading people; and therefore where trade and populousness decrease in a place, our meetings must be expected to grow emptier there' (quoted in Bolam, Goring *et al.* 1968: 176). Moreover the trinitarian controversies indicated, on each side, a high degree of scholarship and learning, reinforced by a series of academies which were established both for candidates for the Dissenting ministry and for lay students. The political climate of the early eighteenth century was far more tolerant than that of the late seventeenth century, when John Bunyan, George Fox and others had earned heroic reputations and experienced persecution. But toleration did not necessarily lead to a decay of piety. As Donald Davie has expertly shown, Dissent in the early Georgian period produced a cultural harvest of devotional literature, of which the poetry of Isaac Watts and Philip Doddridge is the best-known but far from the only examples (Davie 1978: 19–36).

There are, moreover, too many examples within Old Dissent of practices later associated with the Revival for the image of decay to be fully convincing. The itinerancy of Bagshawe and Clegg in Derbyshire has already been mentioned. In the early 1690s the Congregationalist minister Richard Davis launched a revivalist campaign in Northamptonshire. He stressed the danger of sin and damnation, achieved emotional conversions and founded seven new churches. The antagonism which he aroused was based upon his use of lay preachers, his 'invasion' of the pastorates of other Dissenting ministers and the hysteria which his preaching sometimes provoked. All this recurred with the advent of Methodism half a century later. Davis fell foul of opposition from Dissenting ministers of the Presbyterian denomination and his revival was only temporary. But the sentiments which engendered it were widespread among Dissenters as a whole. Dr G.F. Nuttall's research has located numerous instances of personal covenants with God, intensely emotional conversion experiences and the keeping of spiritual autobiographies. The Kidderminster Dissenter Joseph Williams recorded his religious experiences in vivid terms,

while Benjamin Dutton recounted a sermon by the Congregational minister at Ravenstonedale which induced in him a
response characteristic of Methodist converts a generation later: 'I
was so wonderfully melted under a Sense of God's Love, and of
my own Vileness and Sinfulness, that it caused me to cry out in
the Auditory. Which then was a strange, and almost unheard-of
Thing' (quoted in Nuttall 1981: 266). In the west country, notably
in the region of Gloucester, these sentiments were particularly
strong. There is in short sufficient evidence within the older Dissenting denominations of 'intense personal devotion, anchored in
Scripture and the Lord's Supper ... fostered by sermons and Holy
Clubs, finding outlet in ejaculatory prayer, tears and private covenants' (Nuttall 1981: 268) to explain why the Revival did not fall
upon stony ground.

This is one aspect of the tradition of seventeenth-century Puritanism which, in the words of Dr Walsh, was 'still smouldering
away below the crust of conventional piety' (Walsh 1966: 138). It
was a tradition to be found within English Nonconformity and
Scottish Presbyterianism as well as within the Church of England,
and for some it was only just below the surface. This chapter has
tried to show that the Evangelical Revival should not be viewed as
one event which began at Oxford or Aldersgate Street in the mid-
1730s but that its roots were far deeper, more geographically
widespread and more complex than such a short-term approach
might imply. It is only with such an appreciation that one can
hope to do full justice to the events of the 1730s and 1740s.

# CHAPTER FOUR

# The growth of Methodism

The word 'Methodist' itself was not a stranger to the English language in 1730. It signified one who followed specific and orthodox methods, especially in medicine. Dr Johnson's Dictionary defined it, firstly, as 'a physician who practices by theory' and secondly, while referring to its Puritan connotations, as one who professed 'to live by rules and in constant method'. By that time (1755) the term had changed its meaning quite fundamentally; its medical significance was becoming archaic and its primary (and almost exclusive) meaning referred to a specific form of Protestantism. The extent to which it was, in that sense, an unflattering or frankly abusive expression should not be overlooked. It could be applied to anyone who displayed evangelical characteristics. To say that someone had 'turned Methodist' was to castigate the individual concerned as a religious fanatic of unstable mind. When the Norfolk clergyman James Woodforde, noted in his diary that his thatcher, one Harrison, was 'reputed to be a rank Methodist', he was not paying a compliment (Woodforde: II, 113).

Methodism was a term also used more specifically of various new religious groups which emerged as a result of the revival. Only later did it become almost synonymous with the followers of John Wesley. One reason why Methodism, though not the only branch of the Revival, quickly became the best known, may be found in the University of Oxford. 'Methodist' in its religious sense was first applied to the key members of the Holy Club in that university. As well as meeting regularly for prayer and bible-reading, they had earned a reputation for meticulous planning for each hour of the day. They also provided the essential connections whereby the different strands of the Revival were brought together. Without those connections the Welsh revival, for instance, might have remained a separate one. Howel Harris had begun to preach and to form religious societies for his converts in 1735–6; in 1737 he joined forces with Daniel Rowland, relinquished his school-teaching post and embarked upon a remarkable campaign of itinerancy throughout Wales. His societies were sufficiently well organized as to acquire a durable existence independently of his personal presence and by 1750 he had, by establishing a chain of more than 400, created the essence of Welsh Methodism without help from the Wesleys or George Whitefield (Watts 1978: 396–7).

It was Whitefield, however, who by following the examples of field-preaching and the great open air meetings which had been so successful in Wales, helped to extend them to England. Unlike the Wesleys, Whitefield, though an ordained Anglican clergyman, did not come from a clerical family. The son of a Gloucester innkeeper, he was able to study at Oxford University (and hence join the Holy Club) by accepting the lowly status of a servitor, whereby he received an education in return for the performance of menial duties. He experienced an evangelical conversion in 1735, at the age of 21, and thereafter, with that consciousness of 'original sin, or the dreadful consequences of our fall in Adam' which so characterized the early Revival, he preached the 'new birth' (Whitefield *Letters*, 1791/1976: 500). He quickly drew large crowds, among them, no doubt, some of the strongly gospel-minded Dissenters of the west country referred to in the previous chapter. When chided in 1739 for breaches of Church order by the Bishop of Gloucester, Martin Benson, his reply was a curious compound of respect and truculent defiance:

> As for declining the work in which I am engaged, my blood runs chill at the thought of it. I am as much convinced it is my duty to act as I do, as I am that the sun shines at noonday. I can foresee the consequences very well. They have already, in one sense, thrust us out of the synagogues. By-and-by, they will think it is doing God service to kill us. But, my lord, if you and the rest of the bishops cast us out, our great and common Master will take us up. However you

> may censure us as evil-doers and disturbers of the peace, yet
> if we suffer for our present way of acting, your lordship, at
> the great day, will find that we suffer only for *righteousness
> sake* (Whitefield *Letters*, 1791/1976: 501–2).

The truculence was taken even further when Whitefield pointed
out to a local magistrate that 'I know of no law against such meetings as mine' and reminded him that it was his responsibility, as a
justice, to preserve the peace at a forthcoming fair: 'if you do not
this, I shall rise up against you at the great day, and be a swift
witness against your partiality' (Whitefield *Letters*, 1791/1976:
502). It was official hostility of this kind that forced Whitefield into
the fields; he was never a parish priest in England and accordingly
was able to give almost his whole life to international itinerancy.
Much contemporary evidence indicates that he was by far the most
charismatic preacher in the English-speaking world during the
eighteenth century. By a combination of a harmonious voice and
compelling personal presence he gained the status of a star
performer. The element of entertainment and spectacle should not
be disregarded. While professing respect for his fellow-collegian,
Dr Johnson ascribed Whitefield's popularity to 'the peculiarity of
his manner. He would be followed by crowds were he to wear a
night-cap in the pulpit, or were he to preach from a tree'.

Whitefield was quick to appreciate the international ramifica-
tions of the Revival and in 1738 made his first visit to the new
British colony of Georgia. There he helped to found and equip an
orphanage. Georgia was not only the most recent of the thirteen
North American colonies, but was also a prime target for the SPG
(Society for the Propagation of the Gospel), partly because of its
proximity to the Spanish territory of Florida, a base for possible
Catholic expansion. By the mid-1730s, as we have seen, Georgia
was also the home of Protestant refugees from Salzburg. It was a
magnet for would-be evangelists and Whitefield had been preceded by John and Charles Wesley in 1735. There was, however,
one important difference between their respective expeditions.
Whitefield went to Georgia after his conversion; the Wesley
brothers crossed the Atlantic before theirs.

John and Charles Wesley were both sons of the manse; their
father was Rector of Epworth (Lincolnshire) and a High Church-

man who had converted from Dissent. Their dominant and intellectually influential mother also came from a Dissenting background but subsequently adopted High Church opinions. Although life at Epworth was not free from financial constraints, their education was more fortunate than that of Whitefield. John was a pupil at Charterhouse and Charles at Westminster and their access to Oxford was as gentlemen and scholars. John Wesley was a student of Christ Church, the most aristocratic college, and subsequently fellow and tutor of Lincoln. He thus had an academic (and financial) base which he retained until his (catastrophic) marriage in 1751 obliged him, under college rules, to relinquish it. The freedom which this gave him was vital to his future career. His first real exercise of that freedom, as a minister in Georgia under the nominal auspices of the SPG, led him into personal contact with the Moravians, whose legendary serenity on board ship during a storm gave him visible evidence of the reality of faith in God. Although his missionary work in the colony was completely unsuccessful and ended ignominiously after an embarrassing love affair, this encounter with the Moravians had lasting effects.

By the time of Wesley's return from Georgia in 1738 there was a Moravian presence in London. It had been established on the initiative of Zinzendorf after his temporary expulsion from Saxony and grew from Moravian settlements in the Netherlands and from the beginnings of an international missionary operation. In 1738 the Moravian minister Peter Böhler helped to found a society in Fetter Lane, which, while in part an Anglican religious society of the early eighteenth-century type, was predominantly Moravian in ethos. An important link between Wesley and the Moravians was the London bookseller James Hutton, who came from a non-juring family and, though not himself a student there, had known members of the Holy Club in Oxford. He subsequently became one of the first of the English Moravians. He quickly appreciated that the work required female involvement and his marriage (conducted by Zinzendorf) to the daughter of a Swiss Protestant pastor helped to place him at the centre of the Moravian Church's work internationally. It was partly through Hutton, and partly through the German Böhler's famous advice ('preach faith until you have it; and then, because you have it, you will preach faith') that Wesley became more attracted by the Moravians. Hence he went to the City of London to attend their meeting in Aldersgate Street on 24 May 1738, where he felt his heart 'strangely warmed' with a personal sense of assurance that he could trust 'in Christ and Christ alone for salvation ... that He had taken away *my* sins, even *mine*, and saved *me* from the law of sin and death' (quoted in Rack 1989: 144).

It has for long been a matter for debate among historians of Methodism as to whether the conversion of 24 May 1738 was the start of Wesley's career as an evangelical and his previous High Church background was of smaller significance, or whether it was his background which prepared him for his life's work and too much significance should not be attached to that single day. A fair conclusion would stress the importance of both. Many evangelical characteristics were already in place in Wesley's intellectual formation before 1738: the personal asceticism, the sense of accountability to God, the almost obsessive accounting for every moment of time, the Puritanical suspicion of many popular pleasures. The Moravian contact, however, added the sense of personal faith which gave him the certainty that salvation could only be achieved through faith and grace.

It was this sense of the divine blessing upon his preaching that led Wesley to follow Harris and Whitefield into itinerancy and it was the way in which many parish clergy denied him their pulpits that led him to open-air preaching. Early in 1739 he was invited by Whitefield to join him in preaching in the Bristol area and subsequently to replace him there as Whitefield returned to Georgia. Soon Wesley began his famous and successful mission to the unchurched colliers of Kingswood, near Bath, and took over the school which Whitefield had founded for their children. He established a routine which was to last for the rest of his life; travel on horseback, and later by coach, over England, Wales, Scotland (from 1751) and Ireland. He did not omit the Isle of Man. One of his earliest successes was in Newcastle upon Tyne, which, perhaps not coincidentally, had been a Puritan stronghold in the seventeenth century. Here he set up an orphanage, which, though on a minute scale compared with that of Francke at Halle, owed something to that example. In the west country he co-operated briefly with John Cennick, a layman whose family had been

Quaker cloth merchants. In Yorkshire his fellow-member of the Holy Club, Benjamin Ingham, an ordained clergyman who had been with Wesley in Georgia, inspired a separate revival in his native West Riding of Yorkshire. By 1741 Ingham claimed 300 dedicated converts and some 2,000 'constant hearers' (Rack 1989: 217). In the north midlands, David Taylor, a former servant of the Countess of Huntingdon, also preached extensively and founded societies.

Amid the series of independent or semi-independent revivals of the late 1740s it is possible to detect strongly contrasting styles of leadership. Whitefield was not only the star preacher but the most widely-travelled of the English evangelicals. But his frequent transatlantic crossings did not allow him sufficient time to construct a firmly-organized following in Britain and Ireland. That fell to John Wesley, who, though well acquainted with the growth of evangelicalism in parts of continental Europe, went to America only once and concentrated most of his immense energy upon the British Isles. His supreme insight was the perception that Revival could most effectively be sustained and spread by a tightly disciplined connexion linking the new societies together. Wesley, too, became a celebrated field preacher; the painting by Nathaniel Hone depicts him in the open air, almost in the manner of St Francis of Assisi. The transition from the formality of the pulpit to the irregularity of the fields did not come easily to the Fellow of Lincoln College whose intellectual training reflected a certain Oxonian pedantry and rigour. In 1772 he noted in his journal 'To this day, field preaching is a cross to me. But I know my commission and see no other way of "preaching the gospel to every creature"' (Wesley: 22; 348). His principal achievement, however, was in the organization of his adherents in such a way that something resembling a permanent grouping, or sect, emerged. Because of its national nature, it became known as a 'Connexion', responsible ultimately to him. Wherever Wesley preached, local societies developed. These he divided into small 'classes', to which all members belonged, for the spiritual discussion, Bible reading, self-examination and confession of backsliding which were becoming widespread evangelical characteristics. Members who had attained an appropriate degree of holiness were placed in 'bands' for more advanced spiritual improvement.

Wesley recognized that, with only a very small number of ordained Anglican clergymen to support him, he would need to rely heavily upon local lay preachers. The various societies were placed in regional 'circuits' and itinerant lay preachers appointed to each circuit. Their role was a crucial one and, partly because it also drew upon female involvement, proved one of the most controversial aspects of early Methodism. The very notion of a female preacher was one which was alien and somewhat disturbing to eighteenth-century public opinion. It seemed to threaten a reversal not only of the social order but of traditionally-understood gender relationships. It aroused ridicule as well as fear, and Dr Johnson was only articulating a common opinion when he compared a woman preacher to a dog walking upon its hind legs: 'It is not done well; but you are surprized to find it done at all'. Yet a shortage of appropriate lay preachers, as well as of sympathetic clergymen, at times left a vacuum which an articulate woman could fill. In 1771 the Cornish Methodist class leader Ann Gilbert travelled to a nearby village to hear a Methodist preacher; when he did not arrive, she felt inspired to lead the congregation in prayer and to deliver a religious exhortation which amounted to a sermon (Lewis 1995: I, 438). Her success, then and later, in securing conversions led to her unofficial acceptance as a local preacher. John Wesley's response to her preaching was ambiguous. In counselling her with the words 'Sister, do all you can', he fell short of allowing official status to female preachers but implicitly accepted that a movement which relied so heavily upon lay volunteers needed active female support as well.

By the mid-1740s Wesley had organized his followers into a hierarchy of society, circuit, district and (from 1744) a national annual Conference. The Conference consisted of (male) lay preachers selected by Wesley himself and might, without exaggeration, be described as an instrument whereby he maintained an authoritarian control over what he had created. Hence it was Wesley's type of Methodism which survived in England, while that of Whitefield (who died in 1770, 21 years before Wesley) did not. The theological differences between them require separate attention later in this chapter; in the very early 1740s, however, they were colleagues in what to contemporaries was a quite extraordinary series of events.

An aspect of Wesley's authoritarian leadership was a severe restriction of formal membership of his Connexion to those deemed spiritually and morally worthy of such membership. It was not easy to be an eighteenth-century Methodist, Wesleyan or otherwise. Quite apart from external hostility, one had to face the regular examination of one's moral conduct. It was not at all unusual for societies to be purged of the unworthy by expulsions. This helps to explain what might otherwise seem rather small Wesleyan Methodist membership figures. In 1767, the first year for which national figures are available, Wesley could claim only 25,911 members in the entire British Isles (22,410 in England, 2,801 in Ireland, 468 in Scotland and 232 in Wales) (Currie, Gilbert & Horsley 1977: 139). Of course such figures take no account of the followers of Harris and Rowland in Wales or of Whitefield's followers in England. They include only those whose membership was formally defined by payment of a subscription, not the tens of thousands who heard, and were perhaps influenced, by Wesley. But in a population of England and Wales of some seven million and of the British Isles as a whole of some 11.4 million, these membership figures were not large.

Who were the rank and file of Methodists? Ordinary members are notoriously more difficult to identify than leaders. There is evidence that early Methodism made most impact in areas where Anglican provision was at its most limited. Here the problem for the Church of England was not only non-residence but the sheer size of many parishes, especially in the north of England, and the changing pattern of population settlements, which were often at a considerable distance from the parish church. By contrast, many smaller parishes in the south of England, where there was a resident clergyman and often only one main landowner, were often less receptive to Methodism because there was less of a vacuum for it to fill. If there was a developing pattern of Methodist advance, it was one which featured particularly those parishes in upland or forest areas, which were beginning to experience the effects of industrialization and where landownership was not concentrated in the hands of one (possibly hostile) family. Methodism attracted disproportionate numbers from itinerant workers who are sometimes said to have sought in Methodist societies the community spirit which their search for employment had obliged them to leave behind. Early converts included, for instance, soldiers serving in continental garrisons and in the British armies serving abroad in the War of the Austrian Succession (1742–48). Much of the membership was fluctuating and shifting, with occupational migration, backsliding and expulsion; but Methodism also drew upon former members of the pre-1740 religious societies and those who had attended charity schools. They were often the most reliable members.

Dr Field's analysis of occupational status of Methodism shows that in the second half of the century by far the highest proportion (57.5 per cent) were skilled artisans and craftsmen in textiles, manufacturing and mining. The second largest category (16.9 per cent) consisted of labourers, servants and paupers. There was a small but respectable proportion (9.4 per cent) of merchants and other employers; and very few members of the aristocracy or gentry. Methodism, contrary to contemporary belief, was not primarily the religion of the very poor. This impression is reinforced by Dr Watts's survey of 41 of the earliest lay preachers; the skilled artisan category predominates (Watts 1978: 407–9). Dr Field also demonstrates, however, the significant female contribution to early Methodism. Well over half (57.8 per cent) of the English membership between 1759–70 was female, with considerably more single women than single men (Field 1994: 155–67). Methodism was accused at the time of being a disruptive force in family life; possibly the adherence of single women to a Methodist society represented a gesture of self-assertion and independence. On the other hand, it benefited at times from the exercise of more traditional sources of authority and influence. In Georgia both Methodists and Moravians were protected by the military commander and MP James Oglethorpe; the aristocratic patronage of the Countess of Huntingdon was indispensable to Whitefield and many lesser preachers, while the eminent Congregational minister Philip Doddridge, unlike many of his fellow-Dissenters, welcomed Methodists to his Northampton chapel and allowed Wesley access to his pulpit.

Controversy continues over the causes of the Revival in these crucial and dramatic early stages. In 1906 Elie Halévy in his influential *The Rise of Methodism* saw the precipitating factor as one of economic crisis which brought back to the surface the latent

Puritan emotions from the seventeenth century. The winter of 1739–40 was certainly an exceptionally hard one and it was preceded by a poor harvest. Professor O'Brien's index of agricultural prices shows a leap from 92 to 121 between 1738–40 and the increase in the index of grain prices was even sharper, from 92 to 133 (O'Brien 1985: 787–90). A large and sudden increase in the price of food caused considerable hardship and was a familiar source of popular disorder. Such sporadic disorder, however, was frequent in the eighteenth century and the grain riot was an almost legitimate event, revealing more about a customary sense of 'moral economy' and a traditional sense of a 'just' price than about a revolutionary mood or radical departure from the past. The rioting of 1739–40 had numerous precedents, notably in 1710 when a Whig ministry had impeached the High Church Tory Henry Sacheverell, in 1715 with hostility to the Hanoverian dynasty and in Glasgow in 1725 over the Malt Tax. The food riot, too, was hardly a novelty in 1739.

Similarly, the sense of political crisis in 1739–42, with the outbreak of war with Spain, a general election in 1741 and the fall of Walpole had been more than matched in 1702–15. Then there had been extreme bitterness over the succession to the crown, prolonged conflicts between Church and Dissent, and a controversial war, of unprecedented cost, with France over the Spanish empire. The fear of Jacobitism was common to both cases; the rebellion of 1745–6 involved an invasion of England which seemed in December 1745 to be on the verge of success. The effect of that crisis as far as Methodism was concerned was probably two-fold. It heightened the powerful sense of anti-Catholicism which was one of the undercurrents of the Revival; this appears to have been particularly the case in Wales (Jenkins 1978: 195–7). But it also heightened a sense of hysteria about Jacobitism which led to wild accusations of Jacobite sympathy against anyone engaged in unfamiliar activity, including itinerant preaching. Allegations of this kind against Methodists were given plausibility when Wesley's former Oxford colleague John Clayton, a chaplain at the Manchester Collegiate Church, publicly advocated the claims of Prince Charles Edward Stuart, the Jacobite claimant to the throne, when the Jacobite army reached Manchester during the rebellion of 1745. At least some of the vehement anti-Catholicism and anti-

Jacobitism professed by leading Methodists, including Wesley himself, can be explained by an anxiety, born in the 1740s, not to be tarnished with a Catholic or Jacobite image by their detractors.

More convincing explanations for the Revival may, perhaps, be found in the specifically ecclesiastical tensions of the 1730s. In the Parliaments of 1727–34 and 1734–41 Whig anti-clericalism reached an eighteenth-century peak. There were repeated Whig attempts to undermine the authority and property of the Church of England. They took the form, principally, of a Mortmain Act to restrict charitable legacies to the Church and unsuccessful attempts to moderate the tithe system and repeal the Test and Corporation Acts. They were informed by an oppositional Whig mentality which was rationalist and anti-clerical in temper and equivocal about orthodox Christianity. Walpole's attempts to restrain it were only partly effective.

An interpretation of the Revival as a reaction against Whig anti-clericalism is, admittedly, weakened by the hostility of many, perhaps most, Anglican clergymen to early Methodism. But, as against the cool rationalism of the anti-clerical Whigs, Methodism stood for a strongly supernatural form of Christianity which harmonized with a powerfully supernaturalist trait among the population. It stressed the miraculous and the magical and possessed an element of faith-healing. It reconciled interest in science with awe at the power of God; electrical demonstrations, for instance, provided opportunities for enhancing, rather than detracting from, a sense of the divine mystery of the universe. Methodism has been credited with an ability to align itself with, and to build upon, local folk-culture. Upon the fairs and festivals of local communities it superimposed borrowings from the Moravians, such as the lovefeast and watchnight service. In common with the Moravians it had recourse to the casting of lots to seek divine guidance in making vital decisions. In apparently chance occurrences it detected the divine hand – as reward, punishment or warning. It has been suggested that such reasons explain the appeal of Methodism to those who worked in particularly dangerous occupations, notably fishermen, Cornish tin-miners and the Leicestershire coalminers to whom the Countess of Huntingdon's preachers ministered (Welch 1995: 48). In Cornwall, particularly, the experience of industrialization was startlingly new; the mining industry was subject to violent trade fluctuations and those who worked underground were subject to unfamiliar hazards every day (Luker 1986: 609). Evangelical publications frequently published stories of providential escapes from terrifying industrial dangers; the *Arminian Magazine* in 1791 carried an 'Account of a Fire-Damp, in a tin-mine in Cornwall', by the superintendent of the works (*Arminian Magazine:* 14: 579–82). To this consideration may be added the social and religious radicalism of Wesley's advocacy of the community of goods among his followers, in accordance with the practice of the Apostles in the Book of Acts (Walsh 1990: 29–39). The extent to which Wesley's admiration for 'primitive' Christianity was widely shared remains unproven. However, the speculation that, in its early days at least, Methodism profited from a reaction against the commercialization of the age of the South Sea Bubble and the rule of Walpole remains a plausible one.

It is important, however, to avoid any exaggeration either of Methodist unity or popularity. During the early stages of the Revival Methodism in general was dogged by a host of minor controversies and two major ones. These were the split with the Moravians; and the Calvinist controversy.

Wesley's early relationship with the Moravians was extremely harmonious. He visited their settlement at Herrnhut, greatly admired their communal way of living and borrowed or adapted several of their customs. But there were fundamental differences between them. An early sign of conflict came when Cennick broke with Wesley at Kingswood, split the society and took more than half its members with him. During the following five years, Cennick preached throughout Wiltshire, established religious societies and turned them over to the Moravians before embarking on his last great missionary campaign in Ireland. In Yorkshire, similarly, Benjamin Ingham placed his fledgling societies in Moravian hands. By the mid 1740s the Moravians had established a series of well-endowed and flourishing settlements, which achieved economic self-sufficiency and a communal way of life, with segregation of the (unmarried) sexes and a considerable measure of moral regulation. They set up diaconies, or businesses conducted by an official of the congregation for the community as a whole (Hutton 1909: 310). But the Moravian settlement system was in stark contrast to Methodist itinerancy; it encouraged Moravians to abstract themselves from society and live in isolation. At Fulneck, in Yorkshire, the estate of Lamb's Hill was purchased for the Moravians by Ingham and there soon appeared a chapel (1746) and school (1753). Fulneck became the headquarters of the Moravians' Elders' Conference and the centre of a group of adjacent smaller congregations. Other settlements followed at Ockbrook (Derbyshire) and Bedford. With a strict control of membership, an insistence upon uniformity of dress for women and a domination by church officials the settlements remained coherent but inward-looking. A distinguished Moravian historian has called the settlement system 'the road, not to Church extension, but to Church extinction' (Hutton 1909: 314).

Behind these developments, however, there were fundamental differences of doctrine. When Cennick parted company with Wesley he recorded that Wesley had denounced his principles as 'the very opinions of the "still Brethren"' (Cooper 1996: 7). A section of Moravian opinion, strong in the Fetter Lane Society and personified by the Alsatian Philipp Heinrich Molther, adopted the practice of 'being still before the Lord' until they had received assurance of faith and salvation. Molther and others claimed that those who had been converted had no need to observe the 'outward' ordinances of Christianity, notably corporate worship (including communion), prayer, bible reading and good works. Their acceptance in the eyes of God freed them from such requirements and to engage in good works ran the risk of entrapment in the delusion that works themselves could lead to the achievement of saving faith. Dr Podmore has shown that the doctrine of 'stillness' was, in fact, neither an innovation on Molther's part nor a deviation from Moravian practice as a whole. It derived in part from a distaste for the groanings and convulsions which Molther and others encountered in the early days of the Fetter Lane Society and which subsequently gave ammunition to the Revival's critics (Podmore 1994: 83–7). But to John Wesley, 'stillness' seemed an extreme form of 'justification by faith alone'; it was dangerously close to 'antinomianism' – the view that those chosen by God were free from any moral law. Wesley himself strongly attacked this notion. He denounced 'stillness' as derogatory to the ordinances of the Church, on the ground that those ordinances were themselves an essential part of the means to conversion.

The 'stillness controversy' was the occasion for Wesley's withdrawal from the Fetter Lane Society in July 1740. That Society became the embryo of a Moravian congregation and Wesley found a new home at the King's Foundery. He soon entered into theological controversy with the Moravians, asserting that it was possible for an individual to attain to 'Christian perfection' – that is to say, freedom from sin – in this life, by observing the moral law, following the ordinances of the Church and engaging in good works. The Moravians rejected this doctrine, remaining sceptical of the idea that one could 'grow in holiness' and insisting that sin always remained. Dr Podmore has argued that for all his theological differences with them, Wesley still felt an emotional attraction to the Moravians and avoided too close a contact with them, lest it overwhelm him (Podmore 1994: 103–7). At all events, in the later 1740s the Moravian Church in England benefited from a climate of opinion which worked, albeit briefly, in its favour. The validity of its episcopal orders was recognized by Archbishops Wake and Potter, and there was increasing evidence that Moravians were loyal British citizens rather than potential subversives. Their most conspicuous successes lay in the field of imperial, not domestic, missions and in 1749 skilful lobbying secured them an Act of Parliament permitting them to evangelize in the north American colonies. It is true that this Act, by conferring legal recognition upon the Moravians as a separate, and by definition a Dissenting, church, thwarted the ecumenical aspiration of Count Zinzendorf that they might instead become an Anglican 'tropus', or religious order within Anglicanism (Podmore 1994: 268–9). But it gave them a measure of security which was of considerable value in the 1750s, when much anti-Moravian propaganda, some of it based upon the radical excesses of their German settlement of Herrnhaag, some of it the result of financial crises in England, brought them into temporary disrepute. From the 1740s, however, Moravians and Methodists went their separate ways and although Wesley, late in his life, was partly reconciled to the Moravians, the division remained.

The second controversy was more widespread, lasting and damaging. One reason for Cennick's departure from Wesley at

Kingswood was his inclination towards Whitefield's Calvinism rather than Wesley's Arminianism. The difference between the two systems of thought was profound and of long standing. Arminianism, so called after the Dutch Reformed theologian Jacobus Arminius (1560–1609), argued for human free-will, that Christ had died for all mankind and not only for the elect, and that the divine offer of salvation was open to all who would accept it. Many, of course, would not do so and they – deservedly – would be damned. Arminianism accepted completely the principle of original sin and held that humanity, by itself, was too depraved to accept the offer of salvation. But the Arminian position also emphasized the abundance of divine grace, of which all could avail themselves. That grace was believed to operate through the Church's ordinances; hence by a strict observance of those ordinances and by living, as far as possible, a holy life, some people might drag themselves to salvation. John Wesley's specific concept was that of 'prevenient grace', whereby grace is freely available to all and whereby conscience allows the perception of the difference between a sinful and a godly life. As Wesley put it, 'No man sins because he has not grace, but because he does not use the grace which he hath' (quoted in Knight 1992: 26).

To Calvinists, this was tantamount to the 'popish' belief in good works as sufficient for salvation; God alone had the sovereign power to confer salvation, and by that power reserved salvation for the elect. As Calvin himself put it 'God stretches out His hand to all alike, but He only grasps those ... whom he has chosen before the foundation of the world' (quoted in Clifford 1996: 60). The more extreme, or 'hyper', Calvinist position also posited a double decree – of the elect to salvation, of the unregenerate to damnation. Charlotte Bronte in *Jane Eyre* expressed that in its most chilling form through a sermon of St John Rivers:

> Throughout there was a strange bitterness: stern allusions to Calvinistic doctrines – election, predestination, reprobation – were frequent; and each reference to these points sounded like a sentence pronounced for doom (*Jane Eyre*, chapter 30).

To John Wesley, such an attitude negated all effort to secure conversions. Calvinists seemed to teach that men were either saved, irrespective of their sins, or damned, irrespective of their faith and good deeds. Calvinists accused Arminians of making salvation depend on man's free-will, rather than upon God's free grace for the elect; Arminians accused Calvinists of depicting God as unspeakably cruel in condemning some to perdition even before their birth. Each side could cite apparently supporting biblical texts.

The conflict flared into the open in 1739 when Whitefield chided Wesley: 'Is it true that brother Stock is excluded the society [at Kingswood] because he holds predestination? If so, is it right? Would Jesus Christ have done so?' (Whitefield *Letters*, 1791/1976: 499). There followed something of a truce as both leaders appreciated the dangers to Methodism of public wrangling. Wesley, moreover, had to take account of a lesser controversy among some of his lay preachers over his doctrine of 'Christian perfection', whereby those who had been converted and received assurance of salvation were exhorted to seek, partly through 'good works', for a state as close to Christ-like perfection as was humanly possible. Wesley intended this doctrine to operate partly as a protection against backsliding, but a handful of his followers, led by Thomas Maxfield, took it to extreme lengths and revived charges of Interregnum fanaticism by claiming visions, gifts of prophecy and healing and even exemption from death. As a result, Maxfield's followers seceded in 1763, but took barely 200 Methodists with them.

On Whitefield's death in 1770 and the strongly Arminian tone of the Methodist conference in the same year, the Calvinist controversy was resumed. There was a bitter pamphlet war. One of the more interesting protagonists on the Arminian side was John Fletcher (1729–85), a Swiss Protestant by birth, who had signed a covenant with God in his own blood at the age of 15 and had belonged to a 'Holy Club' at the University of Geneva. Having taken Anglican orders and become Vicar of the industrial parish of Madeley in Shropshire, Fletcher proved himself so able a preacher and controversialist that Wesley designated him as his successor as the leader of English Methodism, a possibility ended with Fletcher's premature death in August 1785. When the expulsion of six Calvinistic Methodists from St Edmund Hall, Oxford, in 1768 led the Countess of Huntingdon to set up her own college for the training of Methodist clergy, Fletcher became its Principal. But the clash between the Countess's Calvinistic views and Fletcher's Arminianism soon led him to resign and in the 1770s he wrote several anti-Calvinist tracts under the titles of *Checks to Antinomianism*. Wesley founded the *Arminian Magazine* in 1778 to sustain the onslaught. One problem for him was that most of the Anglican clergy who sympathized with Evangelicalism – Henry Venn, John Berridge, de Coetlogon – were also Calvinists. However, their Calvinism tended to be of a moderate kind, accepting predestination to salvation but not the positive decree to damnation, and some of them played a conciliatory role. A good example is John Newton (1725–1807) who had served on slave ships, was converted in the early 1750s and became an Anglican clergyman at Olney and subsequently in London. That the Calvinist controversy did not become even more divisive was in large part due to such moderating influences. As it was, the main branch of English Methodism, under John Wesley's tight organization, remained Arminian; that in Wales firmly Calvinist.

It remains to consider the intensely hostile emotions which Methodism aroused. Some of it, predictably, came from established Anglican clergy who found their congregations reduced by the competition of Methodist meetings. Some members of the episcopate, including Edmund Gibson, denounced Methodism as 'enthusiasm' – a term of strong abuse, defined by Dr Johnson as 'a vain belief of private revelation; a warm confidence of divine favour or communication' and by Wesley himself as 'religious madness; fancied inspiration'. The Bishop of Exeter, George Lavington, struck a double blow in 1749 with *The Enthusiasm of Methodists and Papists compared*; he raised the joint spectres of mid seventeenth-century anarchy and the feared Catholicism all the more effectively for the recent memory of the Jacobite rebellion. He compared the Methodist class meetings to a type of Confession, accused them of popish superstition and belief in miracles to delude the gullible and the most extreme sexual immorality: 'Many authors have shewn a natural connection between Enthusiasm and Impurity'. Some of the Dissenters took a similar view. The Independent minister Caleb Fleming re-published in 1744 an older tract entitled *A Fine Picture of Enthusiasm ... wherein the dangers of the passions leading in Religion is strongly described* and applied it to 'Modern Methodists'. A theme of such criticisms was that of deception. On Whitefield's death the *Gentleman's Magazine* (40: 1770: 563) commented sourly 'Upon the whole, Mr W.'s imposing upon and *leading captive* so many poor people, his followers and admirers, seems a stronger proof of the weakness of human reason, than any thing he could offer for it'. Even more serious was the charge that this deception involved something close to theft. Judith Milbanke in 1777 complained 'It is a terrible thing when Ldy Huntingdons Preachers get about any body, as if they give their money to *them* & their love to Heaven, it is sufficient to pave their way there, without giving *to or loving* anything else' (Elwin 1967: 81). Some of the early convulsions at Methodist meetings gave credence to such charges, and they were repeated when many local revivals brought renewed outbursts of hysteria in the early nineteenth century.

To this can undoubtedly be added the fear that Methodism threatened the social order by its use of unlettered lay preachers and by its elevation of the religious status of women. The 'priesthood of all believers' was not something which came naturally to someone of Wesley's background, but his dependence on lay people – as preachers, class-leaders, ordinary members and – in the last resort – subscribers meant that Methodism had to give such people a larger role than they would have obtained in any other religious grouping. Wesley's record as a High Church Oxonian ultimately proved reassuring to some of his critics. But – especially in the 1740s – the fear of a re-appearance of a sect which looked suspiciously similar to the alarming Ranters of the mid-seventeenth century accounts for much of the polemic against Methodists in tract and sermon.

Possibly such hostility from the elite helped to stimulate anti-Methodist crowds. The extent to which the eighteenth-century crowd was manipulated from above, or acted spontaneously in articulating genuinely-felt grievances from below, remains a matter for debate. Probably there were elements of both. There is no doubt that local figures of authority helped to stir up popular anti-Methodist feeling and that helps to explain why some lay preachers, such as John Nelson in Halifax, were press-ganged into the armed forces. The level of violence directed against Methodist preachers, mainly – again – in the 1740s is undeniable. Wesley himself was frequently attacked and at least one of his preachers, William Seward, killed by a stone hurled accurately at his head. In June 1741, near Swindon, Cennick and Howel Harris were attacked with mud, sprayed by a fire engine and then 'hindered from preaching' by a mob which 'with guns fired over our heads holding the muzzles so near our faces that we were both black as Tinkers with the powder' (Cooper 1996: 9). Violence was sometimes ignited by the very success of the preachers, especially when the conversion of women seemed to pose a particularly damaging threat to family life. In 1768 a Methodist family in Fermanagh was besieged for two days by a mob hoping to 'starve out' two Methodist preachers who had converted the daughter of another local family (Hempton and Hill 1992: 136).

New converts often faced ridicule from their neighbours. James Hall of Boridge, near Manchester, described how 'some ... would avoid me as though I should spread pernicious contagion around me'. He had to endure such taunts as 'Tell us what the Methodists do in their dark meetings, when they put out the candles?' (*Arminian Magazine*: 1793, 16: 68). Conversions could divide families. The wife of Silas Told of Essex responded to his conversion by exclaiming 'What the d___l possesses you? I hope you have not been among the Methodists. I'll sacrifice my soul rather than you shall go among those miscreants' (Told 1954: 68). Although Told informs us that she later accepted his adherence to Wesley and his work as a teacher at the Foundery-School, it would have been interesting to read her testimony as to the dramatic change in the life of the family as a result of her husband's encounter with Methodism. Deeper passions were at work when Methodists were perceived as killjoys, attacking popular and time-honoured local customs. Wesley was a vehement critic of smuggling. The Cornish Evangelical Samuel Walker of Truro was a particularly severe censor of such customs. Methodism often disapproved of popular recreations. One such, with increasing appeal to the middling orders, was the theatre, of which practically every town of any note was in possession by the 1770s. When advocating the Manchester Playhouse Bill in the House of Lords in 1775 the Earl of Carlisle declared that 'Methodism was daily gaining ground, particularly in the manufacturing towns; and that playhouses, well regulated, would be the means of dispelling those gloomy thoughts, and that melancholy state of mind so favourable to the propagation of the dangerous doctrines embraced by those sectaries' (Stockdale, II: 124). Early Methodism encountered objections of this kind both at elite and popular level and only by making judicious concessions to popular culture did it achieve popular status itself.

It is a testimony to the vitality of Methodism that, despite such hostility, it was transformed between 1740 and 1830 from a relatively minor outbreak of 'enthusiasm' to something approaching a mass movement. Some of the reasons for its growth are apparent in its origins. It appealed in particular to many who had little formal education but who aspired to learn, and who were otherwise denied an active religious role. Its participatory ethos at local level provided an outlet for the articulate but uninstructed. It gave intelligent and spiritually-minded people something worthwhile to do and a sense of belonging. It could deplore the extravagance of the wealthy and advocate the Christian duty of charity without undermining the sanctity of private property. This might help to explain its success among the growing middling and lower middling orders of Hanoverian England. Certainly the newer industrial areas loom large in the rise of Methodism, although its rural counterparts in such key areas as Cornwall were no less important. It has become an academic orthodoxy to observe that Methodism rendered accessible (or 'mediated') the world of learning to those versed in popular culture and absorbed vital elements of that popular culture in return. In the nineteenth century, those closest to that world of learning were the Wesleyans; those closest to popular culture were the Primitive Methodists.

Many Methodists were above the very poorest in the social scale but were sufficiently close to the poverty of others to appreciate its potential consequences for themselves as well as the need for ministration to the less fortunate. The espousal of philanthropy gave Methodism an opening at least to some of the poor, as well as to those who experienced a personal mission to help the poor. Some of the latter were aristocratic grandees, whose influence afforded succour and protection to Methodists at vital moments. Above all, however, Methodism progressed in a society which was still steeped in the supernatural, in magic, in the physical reality of the devil, in the fear of hell. In Methodist preaching there was a strong sense of divine providence, of the working of the divine purpose, of the availability of salvation, of the intervention of God in the material world. It was a message which helped to make sense of a harsh, hostile and otherwise incomprehensible world. Numerous converts claimed supernatural experiences and visions. Silas Told described how, while walking in a remote field, he was struck on the head by an invisible hand 'and looking up, I beheld the sky, as it were, full of the glory of God ... wherein I thought I saw the Lord Jesus, holding both His hands up, from the palms of which the blood seemed to stream down' (Told 1954: 76). It is not surprising that phenomena which are sometimes condescendingly described as 'superstitious' were taken very seriously in a society where life was short, infant mortality high and the likelihood of pain and disease never far away. Methodist revivals existed alongside and sometimes replaced popular festivals which reflected all these 'superstitions'. As Owen Davies notes, it was not the case that Methodism sought to impose superstition upon an increasingly rationalistic population but that the prevalence of superstition was a crucial condition for Methodism's rise (Davies 1997: 264–5). Methodism poses a grave warning against the depiction of Hanoverian Britain as the exclusive domain of materialism and secularization.

# CHAPTER FIVE

# Evangelicalism and authority in the late eighteenth and early nineteenth centuries

Evangelicalism in the later eighteenth century had a somewhat uncertain status in terms of legality. Evangelical parish clergymen in the Church of England, of course, were free to pursue their own style of preaching and pastoral work, although they were unlikely to receive promotion to the highest ecclesiastical rank. Their lay colleagues similarly were not directly inhibited by the law. Dissenting congregations with ministers who espoused evangelical values, though subject to the minimal conditions of the Toleration Act of 1689, had little reason to fear a clash with authority. The various branches of Methodism, however, and particularly that of Wesley, were gradually obliged to define themselves as Anglican or non-Anglican, with the attendant legal consequences of that decision.

John Wesley's own commitment to the Church of England is well known. He deplored the idea of separation from the Church in which he had been raised and which he hoped to re-vitalize from within. He shared much of the traditional Tory suspicion of Dissent. He tried to avoid overt conflict with the Church, for instance by holding meetings at times which did not clash with Anglican services. Charles Wesley was even more hostile towards any hint of secession from the Church. But the problem of definition was rendered increasingly acute by Methodism's shortage of sympathetic Anglican clergymen. Most of those who were sympathetic were effectively debarred by parish duties from itinerancy. Whereas the Revival in Scotland and North America depended heavily on ministers of established churches, that in England, despite its Anglican paternity, did not. Wesley's lay preachers could not administer the communion service. There was pressure from the annual Conference that some of them should be allowed to do so, implying that they should in effect receive separate Methodist ordination. The independence of the American colonies, recognized by Britain in 1783, necessitated new arrangements for any cross-Atlantic movement, since the increasing number of Methodist converts in those colonies were more isolated from the British leadership. Furthermore, as Wesley entered his ninth decade in 1783, the problem of the succession could hardly be postponed.

For all his High Churchmanship, Wesley took a fairly flexible view of Church order. He considered it a reasonable response to changed circumstances when, in 1784, he appointed the Anglican clergyman Thomas Coke as 'superintendent' of Methodists in America, although he was highly displeased when Coke began to call himself a 'bishop' (the Methodist Church in the United States became, and remains, an episcopal church). However, he went much further when he convinced himself that episcopal ordination was not essential for clergymen and that he, as a priest, was entitled to ordain. Armed with this conviction, he ordained three preachers for Scotland in 1785. He justified this step in characteristically plausible fashion, denying any hint of secession or the creation of a new denomination: 'But this is not a Separation from the Church at all. Not from the Church of Scotland, for we were never connected therewith ... nor from the Church of England; for this is not concerned in the steps which are taken in Scotland' (*Arminian Magazine:* 1786, 9: 677). But when Wesley ordained Alexander Mather as a minister in England, a tendency towards separation was clearly under way. Already the Deed of Declaration (1784) had established a new 'constitution' for Wesley's followers, committing the legal charge of the Connexion to one hundred named preachers. By the early 1780s the Countess of Huntingdon's Connexion had been forced out of the Church of England by a litigious clergyman and its meeting houses had to be registered as Dissenting chapels under the Toleration Act.

By the 1780s the first generation of Methodism had acquired considerable respectability. Wesley's own image was that of a venerable patriarch and a champion of order. Both he and Whitefield had expressed some sympathy with the grievances of the

American colonists at the time of the Stamp Act (1765). But in his *Calm Address to our American Colonies* (1775), Wesley strongly condemned the colonial rebels and upheld the claims of the British government to raise taxation; 'fear God and honour the King' was his watchword. At a time of renewed anxiety about public order, with Wilkite disturbances in Britain, this was of considerable importance. The *London Chronicle* of 6–8 November 1770, in a flattering obituary notice of Whitefield, noted that he 'enforced upon his audience every moral duty; particularly, industry in their different callings, and obedience to their superiors; and in a most especial manner loyalty to our amiable Sovereign, never once endeavouring in these distracted times to make a factious use of the great influence he held among his numerous adherents'. Wesley's conference adopted a 'no politics' rule and Wesley argued that his preachers should only 'preach politics' to defend the king and his ministers against 'unjust censures' (*Arminian Magazine:* V: 1782: 151–2). Methodists and Moravians had both won the patronage of Thomas Wilson, Bishop of Sodor and Man, who died in 1755. Wesley, who had been execrated by Bishop Lavington of Exeter in the 1740s, was warmly welcomed to that diocese in 1782 by Lavington's successor but one, John Ross. He was invited to preach in Exeter Cathedral and could appreciate, as Ross's guest, a 'dinner sufficient, but not redundant; plain and good, but not delicate' (Wesley, 23: 250).

The American war undoubtedly contributed to a public perception of evangelicalism generally which was more respectable and conservative than had been the case thirty years earlier. This, perhaps, is one reason why a familiar depiction of evangelicalism in the age of the French Revolution is of a similarly conservative nature, fundamentally law-abiding in principle, and usually in practice. Rather than defying the law, Methodists had exploited it for their own advantage, stressing their legal privileges as members of the established church. In this way they had sought and obtained legal redress when threatened by over-zealous magistrates or by mobs. They had also won the acceptance of many parochial clergy as well as members of the hierarchy. The later years of Wesley's *Journal* give many examples. In August 1784 he preached to 'a crowded audience' at St Andrew's Church, Worcester, where the vicar, William Warmington, told him 'I should be welcome to the use of his church whenever I came to Worcester' (Wesley, 23: 299).

John Wesley died in March 1791, before the more startling developments of the French Revolution had caused serious alarm in Britain. At that time it was still just possible to regard the Revolution as a welcome triumph over absolutism and a severe setback for Britain's principal commercial and imperial rival. Later in the same year Thomas Coke even attempted a Methodist mission in revolutionary France – with singular lack of success (Watts 1995: 6). With the events of 1792–3, however, the Church of England played an increasingly powerful part in opposing the doctrines of the French Revolution as atheistic, republican and anarchical, and in these circumstances it is not surprising that Anglican evangelicals, too, tended to be hostile to French revolutionary thought and to its sympathizers in Britain. The counterattack against the Revolution involved so heavy a deployment of religious argument that it is easy to see why it has been suggested that religion was at the forefront of the British avoidance of revolution in the years 1793–1815.

This opinion has been particularly associated with the French historian Elie Halévy, since the publication of his classic *History of the English People in the nineteenth century* in 1913. Its first volume, a summary of the state of the English people in 1815, sought to answer the oft-repeated question – why was there no revolution in the British Isles at the time when the French Revolution was proclaiming the international nature of its creed and when, moreover, potentially revolutionary groups, such as the United Irishmen and the London Corresponding Society, operated in the dominions of George III? Halévy's explanation placed evangelicalism in its various forms – not only Methodism – at its centre. By drawing on older Puritan traditions, which had already contributed much to the Revival, evangelicalism offered a religious counterpart to oppose the essentially secular and anticlerical ideology of the Jacobins. That Puritan tradition, Halévy argued, could assert quite credibly that traditional liberties, for which seventeenth-century Puritans had fought, were in far more danger from Jacobinism than from any measure which might have been taken by the British state. Evangelicalism, by preaching the sort of conservative values which stressed the spiritual as much as the material needs of the population and the need for respect to be paid to authority, had the effect of discouraging revolutionary agitation as sinful and promoted deference and submission to the existing institutions of the state. In particular the increase of Methodist numbers among the new industrial working classes led to Halévy's conclusion: 'We can watch between 1792 and 1815 an uninterrupted decline of the revolutionary spirit among the sects' (Halévy 1913: 425). This argument, soon hardened into orthodoxy as the 'Halévy thesis', has become so widely repeated that it requires critical consideration in any survey of the Evangelical Revival.

A criticism of the Halévy thesis has questioned its assumption that there was indeed serious danger of revolution in Britain. It needs to be remembered that the post-1789 period, unlike 1848, or, on a smaller scale 1830, was one of French, and not European, revolution. Revolution was only successful outside France where – as in Switzerland, Holland or northern Italy – it was sustained by French arms. Historians such as Jonathan Clark have emphasized the strength of the British 'ancien régime'. In Britain there were already powerful forces which promoted stability; a strong state, a moderately efficient Poor Law reinforced by extensive private charity in times of dearth (Christie 1984: chs III and IV), and a powerful, deep-seated anti-French feeling which had been embalmed in visual art by Hogarth. This approach would stress the minority nature of genuinely revolutionary groups and would point out that the most dangerous types of agitation – in 1794–5 and in 1800–01 – coincided with the worst periods of food shortages. A poor harvest followed by a hard winter – comparable to 1739–40 – caused the index of grain prices to leap from 176 to 227 in 1794–5, and the same index jumped from 167 to 306 in the two years between 1798–1800 (O'Brien 1985: 789–90). The protest this engendered could be interpreted as a traditional crowd response to a sudden and temporary increase in the price of food, rather than an attempt to overthrow the state. Much popular protest was still of a traditional, conservative, 'moral economy' kind, which resisted rather than demanded change and insisted not that constituted authority be overthrown, but that such authority exert its lawful power to fend off the worst material hardships. The Irish rebellion of 1798, though a serious threat to internal security, was caused by factors which hardly applied in Britain. Moreover, much of the anti-revolutionary propaganda of the 1790s emanated not from evangelicalism but from traditional Anglican political theology which stressed obedience to divinely-constituted authority. It has been shown that Burke's *Reflections on the Revolution in France* (1790) drew heavily on this source (Clark 1985: 249–58). Some of the most outspoken proponents of High Church Anglicanism were in fact suspicious of evangelical lay preaching as potentially subversive. Richard Mant, Rector of All Saints, Southampton, saw in evangelical itinerancy not a pro-phylactic against revolution but a return to the disorder of the Commonwealth period (Lovegrove 1988: 19). At the popular level, anti-Methodist mob activity continued spasmodically, usually in areas of new revival, such as Cornwall (1781), Yorkshire (1790s) and Nottinghamshire (1790s). Such disturbances were sometimes linked to high food prices and resentment at the solicitations of the lay preachers for financial contributions (Hempton 1996: 160).

A second argument against the Halévy thesis concerns evangelical numbers. The population of the British Isles at the time of the first official census of 1801 has been computed as 15,846,000 (England 8,479,000; Wales 541,000; Scotland 1,610,000; Ireland 5,216,000). In this context the number of Methodist members looks minuscule indeed; in 1791 there were 72,476, including Ireland (Rack 1989: 437). In the same year, the Methodist Conference was informed that there were 218 lay preachers in England and Wales, 17 for Scotland, 68 for Ireland, 12 for the West Indies and nine for Canada (*Arminian Magazine:* XIV: 1791: 489–94). Wesleyan Methodist membership in 1801, the year of the census, was no more than 87,010 in England (with a further 4815 for the New Connexion); the figure for Ireland was 24,233, for Wales 1178, for Scotland 1341. By the time of the second census, in 1811, total Methodist membership in the British Isles was just over 181,200 in a population of 18,044,000 (Currie, Gilbert & Horsley 1977: 140). It would be difficult, at face value, to attribute so profound a political influence to one per cent of the population. On the other hand, Methodism continued to grow more rapidly than the population as a whole. In 1794 and 1795, years of exceptionally high food prices, Wesleyan Methodist membership grew by 13.52 per cent and 8.30 per cent respectively (Currie, Gilbert &

Horsley 1977: 40). In some areas, naturally, Methodist membership was higher than the national average (three per cent of the
population of Manchester in 1801, over five per cent of the population of Cornwall in 1824). The number of adherents and
hearers, even if the cautious estimate of two per member is accepted, was in the region of 210,000–300,000 by 1800 (Rack 1989:
437–8). Moreover, Halévy ascribed the avoidance of revolution to
evangelicalism as a whole, and not only to Methodism. But the
relevant numbers are none the less small, even if it could be
assumed that all concerned were preaching the values of conservatism, order and deference.

Of course, that assumption cannot be made. A third critique of
the Halévy thesis stresses the variety of opinions among evangelicals, within the Church, among Methodists and among the older
Dissenting sects. John Wesley himself, while a pillar of political
conservatism, held views about personal wealth and property
ownership which were heavy with radical implications. He was
attracted by the community of goods practised by the early apostles, deplored the growing affluence of many of his followers
towards the end of his life and quite deliberately pitched his
appeal to the poor. Dr Walsh, indeed, has commented on Wesley's
extraordinary courtesy to the poor: 'he saw in the beggar the
awesome image of the suffering Christ' (Walsh 1994: 16–17).
Although he was no democrat, and did not favour political rights
for the poor, he compared their moral qualities favourably with
those of many of the elite. This, as Dr Walsh observes, was hardly
the attitude of one whose objective was to inculcate submission to
the capitalist work ethic.

Beyond Wesley himself, many of his preachers embraced what
were by the standards of the time quite radical ideas. Samuel
Bradburn of Manchester and John Pawson were hardly uncritical
apologists for the old order and some lay preachers embraced
doctrines of the rights of man associated with Thomas Paine.
Seven Methodists belonged to the radical Society for Constitutional Information in Sheffield and others in the mid-1790s
supported the London Corresponding Society (Watts 1995: 358).
Within Methodism there was tension between 'Church Methodists', who deplored any break with the Church of England and
'Methodist Dissenters' who believed that such a break was an

acceptable price for the maintenance of their accepted practices. The latter element contained some feeling of anti-clericalism, a democratic urge which claimed that the lay preachers should be allowed to administer communion, and that this office should not be reserved to the few ordained Anglican clergy among the followers of Wesley (Walsh 1965: 286–7). Some Methodists wished to take these democratic, egalitarian instincts to the point of departure from the Church.

In the mid-1790s a group of radical Methodists led by Alexander Kilham (1762–98) did precisely that. Kilham, already a supporter of parliamentary reform, as Wesley had never been, campaigned vigorously for the right of local Methodist societies to have the communion in their own meeting-houses and from their own preachers, rather than from the parish priest. The 'Plan of Pacification', agreed as a compromise by the Methodist Conference in 1795, allowed this practice in meeting-houses where a majority of trustees, stewards and class leaders favoured it. This did not deter Kilham's agitation, and he was expelled by the Conference in 1796. His 'Methodist New Connexion' attracted some support in Yorkshire, Nottinghamshire and Lancashire (it was particularly strong in Ashton-under-Lyne) and numbered almost 8,000 by 1815 (Watts 1995: 359–63). This first radical secession from the mainstream of Wesleyan Methodism was followed by a second, more serious, breakaway in 1808, when a group of Methodists in Cheshire and Staffordshire held a series of dramatic and well-publicized camp meetings, of which the best-known took place at Mow Cop on 31 May 1807. It was attended by several thousand persons and witnessed some of the convulsions and hysteria which had accompanied early Methodism sixty years earlier. The transatlantic connection was emphasized by the involvement of the American evangelist Lorenzo Dow. Conscious of the need for respectability, the Wesleyan Methodist Conference condemned camp meetings, and when their chief organizer, Hugh Bourne, refused to abandon them, he, like Kilham, was expelled. In 1811 his 'New Meeting Methodists' united with the followers of the radical Staffordshire Methodist William Clowes of Tunstall to form the Primitive Methodists. The word 'primitive' signified a desire to return to an original purity, uncorrupted by subsequent accretions, just as 'primitive Christianity' indicated a wish to return to the supposed purity of gospel times. The Primitive Methodists' numbers were small, although they had risen to 25,000 by 1821 (Currie, Gilbert & Horsley 1977: 140). Their strength lay mainly in the north of England and their membership was more obviously working-class in composition than that of the Wesleyan Methodists. They placed less emphasis, too, upon a clerical elite. For all their relatively small numbers, the New Connexion and the Primitive Methodists reveal that Methodism – let alone evangelicalism more generally – was not a monolithic block with a uniform political outlook.

As originally propounded, then, the Halévy thesis is at best not proven. But it has been adapted and re-worked by other historians to accommodate new evidence and the question of the potentially anti-revolutionary role of evangelicalism remains a pressing one. Most significantly, perhaps, E.P. Thompson, in *The Making of the English Working Class*, though making few specific references to Halévy, takes much of his argument seriously. For Thompson, Methodism might well have included radicals within its ranks, but its main impact upon working people was a negative, culturally repressive, one. It offered a distraction from radical politics and served only as 'the chiliasm of despair' – meaning a sense of the imminence of the second coming – for those suffering the worst effects of the industrial revolution. By offering an other-worldly alternative to the austere realities of daily existence, the allegation goes, evangelical religion, and Methodism in particular, indoctrinated its adherents into a state of mind in which they would the more easily submit to the discipline of the factory and coal-mine. Methodism, according to Thompson, 'appears as a pitiless ideology of work', inculcating a deep sense of sin and shame. He is particularly hard upon evangelical Sunday Schools which, instead of providing genuine educational advance through the promotion of literacy, committed 'psychological atrocities', the sole purpose being to prepare children for the world of work (Thompson 1963: 375–9). Although the author concedes that practice in Methodist Sunday Schools varied considerably, the overall impression conveyed is one of suppression of initiative and the breaking of the will by the inculcation of guilt. One might be forgiven for detecting in the author's highly colourful and emotive language – 'the perverted eroticism of Methodist imagery', 'Sabbath orgasms of feeling', 'psychic exploitation' (Thompson 1963: 369, 370, 375) – some kind of personal grievance against all things evangelical.

As we have seen, however, Methodism did not recruit its greatest numbers from the very poorest. Nor did the other evangelical groupings. A.D. Gilbert has shown that by far the largest occupational group within Wesleyan Methodism between 1800 and 1837 was that of the artisans, at 62.7 per cent. The comparable figure for Primitive Methodists was 47.7 per cent, for Baptists and Congregationalists 63 per cent and for nonconformity as a whole 59.4 per cent (Gilbert 1976: 63). Even when allowance is made for the male predominance in calculations of this kind, it is clear that a very high proportion of rank and file evangelicals were skilled workers or independent craftsmen, that is to say those whose skills could command the highest wages in the labour market. It is true, of course, that the skilled craftsman was vulnerable to trade cycles – as, indeed, was the shopkeeper and manufacturer – but it was not principally to such people that the 'chiliasm of despair' applied. By contrast, Gilbert's figures show that the proportion of members who were labourers and colliers was far lower: 17.1 per cent for Wesleyans, 28.6 per cent for Primitive Methodists (confirming their higher, but not overwhelming, proletarian profile), 6.0 per cent for Baptists and Congregationalists and 17.4 per cent for nonconformity as a whole (Gilbert 1976: 63). Dr Lovegrove's recent conclusion about the evangelical Dissenters in the 1790s dismisses the 'chiliasm of despair' and sees the increase in their numbers as springing from 'a sense of social and material progress rather than failure' (Lovegrove 1988: 20).

Methodism contained, moreover, a considerable degree of ideological diversity. The will of the Conference should not be taken for the practice of the locality. The Wesleyan Connexion combined an apparently authoritarian structure with much local fluidity. The repeated revival movements in early nineteenth-century Cornwall, for example, with their powerful emotionalism and open appeals to the supernatural were frowned upon, but not extinguished, by the Conference (Luker 1986: 606–7). The dependence upon lay preachers, class leaders and other helpers, both male and female, rendered Methodism so obviously a voluntarist body that the goodwill of its volunteers could not be alienated. The experience of Quakers and Moravians showed that strong internal discipline, accompanied by many expulsions and perhaps consistent with notions of 'repression', tended to be accompanied by a very small membership. Admittedly, the Wesleyan form of Methodism subsequently became, of all the nineteenth-century Dissenting denominations, that which most resembled the Church of England. With its own ordinations and theological college Wesleyanism became by the 1830s a firmly organized denomination under the strict leadership of Jabez Bunting (1779–1858). He sought harmonious relations with the Church of England and disliked political radicalism. He elevated the authority of the Pastoral Office within Wesleyanism at the expense of more popular, lay, initiatives. Bunting's reputation has been savaged by historians (for example, Ward 1972: 20). But even if depictions of him as a conservative autocrat are accepted, it needs to be remembered that his years of dominance were somewhat later than those analyzed by Thompson. Moreover, Bunting did not speak for all Methodists. The religious census of 1851 listed no fewer than seven separate branches of Methodism (the Original Connection; the New Connection; the Primitive Methodists and four smaller groups) together with two branches of Calvinistic Methodism.

The difficulties which arise from treating the political conservatism of Bunting as representative even of Wesleyan Methodism has been pointed out by A.D. Gilbert. Contending that one must look far beyond the official pronouncements of the Conference and the Wesleyan establishment in the early nineteenth century, Gilbert claims that the real world of Methodism and of evangelical Dissent more generally is to be found in the culture of chapel life at local level. Here, the picture is one of religious 'deviance', with a conscious rejection of the Church of England and a substantial measure of political radicalism. So pervasive was the association of religion and politics, and so closely linked were the Church of England and the constitution of the state that non-Anglican groups almost automatically incurred suspicion of disaffection. Gilbert detects in the Methodist chapel culture of the Peterloo period an anti-establishment egalitarianism, a defensive determination to preserve civil liberties (especially freedom of preaching and worship) and a highly critical attitude towards alleged abuses of state power. Overall, however, 'Methodists and Dissenters ... were radical in a moderate sense', sympathetic to social protest but never straying into illegality (Gilbert 1979: 391–2). Although he rejects the predominantly conservative portrayal of Methodism and evangelical Dissent depicted by Halévy and Thompson, Gilbert none the less regards evangelicalism as a source of political stability. He does so by emphasizing that the moderate and firmly non-revolutionary nature of this radicalism acted as a 'safety valve' for the relatively harmless release of passions which, if pent up, could have taken a direction much more dangerous to the state. Gilbert adds the telling point that Methodist strength was disproportionately high in those regions where the early stages of the industrial revolution posed the most serious threat to the social order. Instead of one per cent of the population, it is more accurate 'to think of something approaching 20 per cent of the most politicized section of the adult "lower orders" being associated with chapel communities' (Gilbert 1979: 395–6). Methodism therefore emerges as a potentially reforming movement on a numerically significant scale. In that sense it might indeed have contributed to Britain's avoidance of revolution, if not for the reasons suggested by Halévy. Such a view would have been recognizable to older historians, such as R.F. Wearmouth, who saw Methodist lay preaching and chapel stewardship as the training ground for future leaders of Chartism and trades unions.

Dr Gilbert's interpretation is open to the objection that early nineteenth-century England (and probably Britain) was sufficiently stable as to render inappropriate the comparison to a boiler which would have exploded without the essential safety valve. It has also been observed that the political issues in which chapel communities took most interest were the defence of their own religious freedom, the promotion of anti-slavery and opposition to Catholic emancipation, rather than such obvious radical causes as parliamentary reform. Much energy was spent on internal conflict over preachers, Sunday schools and forms of worship (Hempton 1995: 24). The most radical opinions of all were expressed by the sections of Dissent which were strongly resistant to evangelicalism. Some Unitarians, notably Joseph Priestley, openly sympathized with the French Revolution and thus brought all Dissenters under suspicion at a time of heightened governmental nervousness. But Gilbert's conclusions about the 'moderate radicalism' of evangelicals outside the Church are supported by evidence that those Dissenters who possessed the franchise were increasingly inclined to vote for candidates of the Whig opposition who looked for inspiration to Charles James Fox (Phillips 1982: 292ff). Although Fox's name was struck from the Privy Council after he had publicly toasted 'the Sovereignty of the People of Great Britain', his form of radicalism, and that of his party, was of a moderate and genteel kind. Similarly, the willingness of Dissenters to pursue their aspirations through the constitutional mode of elections and other forms of parliamentary pressure indicates a non-revolutionary approach to politics in an electoral system which, as Frank O'Gorman and others have demonstrated, was a good deal more accessible and representative than has always been appreciated.

The numerical impact of the Revival is best appreciated when its effects upon the older Dissenting sects are considered. It has often, and rightly, been observed that although the revival emanated in the first place from the Church of England, Protestant dissent was the ultimate beneficiary. The former followers of Whitefield were of the utmost importance here. His failure to organize them into a Wesleyan-style connexion left many of them to associate with the Independent, or Congregational, denomination, where a shared Calvinism made them welcome. But an even more important consideration was that the Independents and Baptists, from about 1780, began to adopt the practice of itinerancy, to branch outwards from their rather enclosed chapels and communities. As a result, they greatly increased their membership. The number of Nonconformist congregations increased tenfold between 1773 and 1851 (Watts 1995: 23–4). It has been estimated that the numbers of Congregational adherents rose from 35,000 to 127,000 between 1800 and 1838 and those of the particular Baptists rose from 24,000 to 86,000 in the same period (Gilbert 1976: 37). Behind these increases lay fundamental changes. As Dr Lovegrove has revealed, a much earlier Nonconformist tradition of itinerant preaching was resuscitated on a national scale. More and more Independent and Baptist ministers sought to combine the roles of resident pastor to a flock and touring preacher within a local radius. Whereas Methodist preachers were regularly moved from circuit to circuit, their Dissenting counterparts tended to adhere on a long-term basis to the same area. John Hill, the Independent minister of Ravenstonedale, Westmorland, established such a circle, as did the Baptist John Palmer of Shrewsbury in Shropshire and central Wales (Lovegrove 1988: 44–4, 89). In Nailsworth, Gloucestershire, the Shortwood Baptist Church underwent a spectacular increase in membership under the pastorate of Benjamin Francis in the forty years after 1758. Francis preached extensively in neighbouring parishes and was aided by a spirit of tolerance on the part of local Anglicans, who responded to his type of evangelicalism by seeking not to repress but to emulate it. He was also aided by a pattern of landownership which was highly diversified, and where it was impossible for the hostility of a single dominant gentry family to use its local power and patronage to impede the advance of evangelical Nonconformity. (Urdank 1990: 85–96).

The relationship between evangelicalism and authority in Scotland took a very different form. The formal membership of Wesleyan Methodism remained low. It was 1,041 in 1800, 3,903 in 1830 and only 3,604 in 1840 (Currie, Gilbert & Horsley 1977: 139–40). No doubt the Calvinist tradition of the Presbyterian Church in Scotland did not always find Wesley's Arminianisn entirely congenial. But Methodism was far from the principal vehicle for the revival in Scotland. For evangelicalism won much support within the Presbyterian Church itself. In the later eighteenth century, evangelicals within the Kirk had been the 'popular' and reforming party, critical of lay patronage of church livings and of the ecclesiastical establishment. These popular roots were to be of considerable significance. In 1811 the minister of the Fifeshire parish of Kilmany, Thomas Chalmers (1780–1847) underwent a series of personal crises which led to an evangelical conversion. It had dramatic results far beyond his own neighbourhood: 'for many, his conversion became a symbol for the Evangelical revival in Scotland' (Brown, S.J. 1982: 50). He had read Scott's *The Force of Truth* and Wilberforce's *Practical View*. His early associates included the son of William MacCulloch of Cambuslang.

Chalmers soon drew large audiences and demands for his preaching in other parishes virtually turned him into an itinerant. As with so many evangelical preachers, his success has been attributed in part to his own histrionic abilities. But there was also a sentimentality in his mode of address which appealed to the fashionable Romanticism among his middle and upper-class hearers, while a certain polished elegance of phrase ensured that he maintained his links with polite society in Edinburgh (Brown, S.J. 1982: 58–9). Chalmers preached a type of moderate Calvinism which, while stressing man's depraved state, did not over-emphasize the double decree of election and reprobation. Indeed his Calvinist orthodoxy was sometimes questioned. After 1811 he became a powerful figure within the Church of Scotland and helped to move it in an evangelical direction. He was the driving force behind the Church extension campaign of 1834–41, helping to create more than 200 new parish churches, mainly in new industrial areas (Brown, S.J. 1982: 373). His promotion of social reform through the concept of the 'godly commonwealth' made evangelicalism in Scotland accessible well down the social scale. He had hoped to achieve this ideal through the established church. But his championship of the bitterly controversial issue of the right of congregations to choose their own ministers contributed to the great Disruption of 1843, when more than a third of its ministers left the Church of Scotland. They formed the Free Presbyterian Church, of which Chalmers was the first moderator. This was symptomatic of the emergence of a marked pluralism in Scottish religious life during the nineteenth century. Dissent in Scotland developed at a relatively late stage, but very rapidly, between c. 1790 and 1843. This was a pluralism in which evangelical religion could flourish, outside as well as within, the state church. The revival in Scotland owed far more to McCulloch and Chalmers than to Wesley.

The revival in Ireland bore much more markedly the imprint of Methodism. The membership of Wesleyan Methodism doubled between 1791 and 1815 (from 14,158 to 29,357), with spectacular increases in 1800 and 1801, while the total of Wesleyan and Primitive Methodists reached 36,903 in 1830. A high proportion of these members, however, was concentrated in two relatively small areas, the 'linen triangle' of Ulster and the 'Lough Erne rectangle' (Hempton 1996: 36–43). Much of this growth may be attributed to the success of itinerancy among Protestant communities. It attracted wide notice. A reviewer in the *Gentleman's Magazine* (LXXV, 1805: 150) complained that 'it seems Ireland, like Great

Britain, is overrun with itinerant preachers, who glory in the conversion of the Catholicks; and one of them ... says "It bears strongly on my mind that, when we are about *seven times* round the island, *the walls of Babylon will come tumbling down*" '. There were indeed strenuous efforts on the part of 'a host of evangelical societies' to convert large sections of the Irish Catholic population (Hempton & Hill 1992: 60–1). In this endeavour they were almost entirely unsuccessful. As in other parts of the world, Catholicism in Ireland remained largely resistant, and often hostile, to evangelicalism, especially when its proselytizing societies were sponsored by English evangelicals or Anglo-Irish landlords. Many such organizations were associated with the evangelical missionary societies which were beginning to appear in England and Scotland. What is notable about the revival in Ireland between 1770 and 1830 is what two leading authorities have called 'its lack of denominational and doctrinal homogeneity' (Hempton & Hill 1992: 15). There was a significant, if relatively small, evangelical element among the clergy of the established Church of Ireland, while the Wesleyan and Calvinistic versions of Methodism both made considerable headway in Ulster. But there were limits to the possibilities of expansion. The religious revival of 1859 was largely an Ulster phenomenon, and one of the longer-term consequences of evangelicalism in Ireland was to re-affirm the Protestant identity of that province.

In England, there were specific theological reasons why the revival particularly affected the Independents and the New Connexion of the General Baptists, who had broken away from their parent body and its Unitarian doctrines, in 1770. While the effect on the Quakers came later, only the old Presbyterian denomination, which had become almost completely Unitarian and rejected most evangelical teaching, was unaffected. The revitalization was made possible by a tempering of the older 'high', or 'hyper' type of Calvinism, which had insisted upon the double predestinarian decree of salvation and damnation. The Calvinism which prevailed in the later eighteenth and early nineteenth centuries, both among Anglican Evangelicals and most of the Dissenters, was of a more moderate kind. It avoided a stress on the notion that some were irrevocably destined to perdition. The Cambridge Evangelical Charles Simeon claimed that 'the Calvinists in general do not believe the doctrine of absolute reprobation', while Henry Venn declared himself 'no friend to high Calvinism ... predestination cancels the necessity of any change, and dispenses at once with all duty' (Walsh 1997; Venn 1834: 32). This type of Calvinism was not inconsistent with preaching the gospel to all, and conversion could be regarded as evidence of a person's election to salvation, as well as the fulfilment of the divine plan. A key text, though by no means the first, in this process was *The Gospel worthy of all Acceptation* (1785) by the Cambridgeshire Baptist Andrew Fuller. In this theological climate a series of mission societies sprang up: the Baptist Missionary Society (1792), the non-denominational (but firmly evangelical) London Missionary Society (1795), the British and Foreign Bible Society (founded on the initiative of the Welsh Calvinistic Methodist Thomas Charles in 1804) and the (Wesleyan) Methodist Missionary Society in 1813. Irish branches of the Church Missionary Society and of the Methodist Missionary Society were founded in 1814 and 1817 respectively. The sense of missionary optimism was enhanced by reports of successes (and heroic failures reminiscent of martyrdom) from overseas and the achievement of a major evangelical objective, the abolition of the British slave trade in 1806–07.

The mission societies not only gave an added incentive to evangelical organization through the need for fund-raising and the interest in the progress of missionary work. They also turned some of their attention to the domestic scene. In 1795 the Baptist Missionary Society resolved to use some of its funds for domestic purposes and two years later there was founded the Baptist Society for the Encouragement and Support of Itinerant and Village Preaching (Lovegrove 1988: 25). Their efforts meant that the proportion of non-Anglicans in Britain was growing. But missions were viewed suspiciously by many in authority lest they foment slave or colonial uprisings overseas and sedition at home. The East India Company in particular resisted them.

Indeed, important sections of the governing elite regarded evangelicalism as a force for instability. Its democratic implications caused particular concern. The Church of England was increasingly on the side of authority and no longer felt threatened, as in the 1730s, by an anti-clerical Whig establishment. George III was one of the most firmly Anglican of English monarchs, while the ministries of Lord North (1770–82) and William Pitt the Younger (1783–1801; 1804–6) treated the Church as a bulwark of the constitution. At the local level, many Anglican clergymen had profited from the parliamentary enclosure movement and from the commutation of tithes in kind (often difficult to collect) for a cash payment. Their improved financial and social status was reflected in the growing number of clergymen who became magistrates. In 1762 only two of the 192 Justices of the Peace in Norfolk had been clergymen, while in 1831 the figure was 78 of 204 (Jacob 1982: 431). It has been suggested that, as magistrates charged with the task of enforcing the law against poaching, trespassing and petty theft, the clergy came into a heightened state of conflict with the rural poor. In such circumstances, popular movements of any kind were unlikely to be well received in clerical circles, especially in the light of the spoliation of the French Church by the revolutionary regime in the 1790s.

In the face of such unease about their political loyalty, it was not surprising that Methodist leaders in particular should have insisted repeatedly upon their essential respectability. Dr Whitehead, in his funeral sermon for John Wesley, asserted that the influence of Methodists was 'friendly' and would 'have a tendency to peace and good order' (Whitehead 1791: 53). Thomas Coke assured the prime minister, Lord Grenville, in January 1807 that Wesleyan Methodists, like Dissenters as a whole, were 'a very large Body of the second and third Orders of the People'; they were 'a truly loyal People from both principle and affection' (BL Add MS 59307, f. 197). Perhaps they were protesting too much. Methodist professions of loyalty to King and constitution, which at face value give some support to the Halévy thesis, should always be understood as part of a defence mechanism against attacks upon their good citizenship.

The need for such a defence became apparent as there were moves at the turn of the century to curb itinerant preaching by amending the Toleration Act of 1689. This measure, under which Dissenting ministers and schoolmasters could obtain licences to preach and teach, was regarded by Dissenters and by many Methodists as a cornerstone of English liberties. But from the 1790s, public agitation in Britain, and rebellion in Ireland, raised fears in Parliament and among some Anglican bishops that itinerant preaching could have subversive effects, especially as it was alleged that many of these itinerants were uneducated and barely literate. Samuel Horsley, Bishop of Rochester, thought that Methodism was a refuge for radicals whose overtly political campaigning had been thwarted by the 'two Acts' (the Seditious Meetings and Treasonable Practices Acts) of 1795, which had greatly restricted the legal size of public meetings (Watts 1995: 368). Some of those who associated itinerancy with dangerous radicalism sought to exclude itinerants from the protection of the Toleration Act. They argued that a restriction of the issue of licences under that Act to the ministers of well-established congregations, who could demonstrate a respectable educational level and provide testimonials as to their moral character from other ministers, would sharply curb the numbers of unlettered itinerants.

The Whig MP Michael Angelo Taylor put forward a bill to this effect in 1800 and withdrew it only at a late stage and partly as a result of Pitt's refusal to support it. There is evidence that Pitt was influenced in his decision by his Evangelical friend William Wilberforce. But in 1810, four years after Pitt's death, a more formidable attack upon popular preaching was made. This time its proponent was Lord Sidmouth, a former prime minister (as Henry Addington) and a future Home Secretary. His complaint was that the number of preachers' licences had greatly increased over the previous decade and that many of them had been issued to illiterate men who had been able, armed with a certificate of legality, to challenge the clergy. Although a few well-educated Dissenters endorsed it, Sidmouth's bill encountered powerful opposition from the representative organizations of the Dissenting denominations and from the newly-formed Wesleyan Committee of Privileges. Some 700 petitions against the bill reached Parliament and they were supported by prominent Whig peers such as Lord Holland. When Sidmouth introduced his bill in the House of Lords in May 1811 he received so little encouragement that it was lost without a division (Davis 1971: 148–69). The impetus of the petitions was such that in the following year (1812) the Five Mile and Conventicle Acts, survivals of the Restoration era when Dissent was technically illegal, were both repealed.

One of the most significant features of the campaign against

Sidmouth's bill was the way in which evangelical and non-evangelical Dissent were able to combine effectively. A threat to religious liberty brought Methodism and the older Dissent into political alliance for the first time. There could be no doubt thereafter that the Methodist groups in England were Dissenting denominations. At the same time the Calvinistic Methodists both in north and south Wales, who had been able to rely to a greater extent than their English counterparts upon clergy of the established church, also formally seceded. Thereafter, evangelicalism had less to fear than previously from the law, despite the occasional vexatious prosecution. For it is also noteworthy that the campaign of 1811 was conducted entirely along constitutional lines, strictly within the limits of the law. Such was their confidence in the existing legal and political system that evangelicals (and other Dissenters) were prepared to make full use of the courts and of traditional methods of seeking parliamentary redress. In the nineteenth century, evangelicalism outside the Church of England enjoyed freedom of worship, although not, initially, full civil equality with Anglicans. Those inside the Church, however, both clergy and laity, did not suffer such a handicap and made their own distinctive contribution to public life.

# CHAPTER SIX

# The wider impact of the Evangelical Revival

The Revival took place at a time of competition for the allegiance of the subjects of all the régimes which have featured in this book. The rivalry between Catholic and Protestant gave rise to an out-pouring of propaganda, much of it printed, some of it visual, in ceremonial or architectural forms, much of it at a popular level, relying on prints and cartoons. In Britain, the rivalry between Whig and Tory, between Hanoverian and Jacobite, and in America the rivalry between rebel and loyalist, also necessitated a propaganda battle. The struggle for allegiance was intensified by the French Revolution and its lengthy aftermath. One has a sense thereafter of a conflict of ideas between religion and irreligion, and between different (and frequently mutually hostile) religious traditions. Promoters of the Evangelical Revival, therefore, were among many who sought to persuade, influence and convert.

We have seen that a print culture, and an assumption of wide-spread literacy, lay behind the international linkages between the separate revivals. In England, the (admittedly questionable) sig-nature evidence suggests a male literacy level of some 45 per cent in 1715 and 60 per cent in 1760; and a female literacy level of 25 per cent for women in 1715 and 40 per cent in 1760, with possible higher figures for Scotland and the New England colonies. It may be reasonable to assume that more than half of the population of Britain had some command of reading by the 1770s and that many who do not appear as literate in the statistics produced by sig-natures in the marriage register had some kind of indirect access to the printed word. There is, of course, always the danger that, by reason of its very survival, the printed source will be given disproportionate attention by historians. An oral culture was also essential to religious proselytizing. A striking example of the evangelical preacher who possessed hardly any formal education was the Yorkshire miner Dan Taylor, an ex-Methodist whose fervent Arminianism led to the formation of the General Baptist New Connexion in 1770 and to its early successes in the midland counties.

The spoken and the printed word were probably of approximately equal importance in the diffusion of evangelical ideas. As we have seen, the printed sermon, the revival narrative, the autobiographical fragment and the published journal of a revivalist leader were all crucial means of communication. Much depended upon the ability to popularize traditional Christian teaching as expressed in theological classics. This was the purpose of John Wesley's *Christian Library*, 'a Reader's Digest of spirituality', whereby he brought celebrated religious authors, in abbreviated and accessible form, to his adherents (Walsh 1994: 9). Of particular importance was the religious periodical. The *Arminian Magazine* and its successor the *Methodist Magazine*, together with the *Evangelical Magazine* (which was more inclined in a Calvinist direction) in the early nineteenth century, provided a variety of memoirs, poetry, reports from foreign missionaries, letters, accounts of the annual Conference and short summaries of newly-published religious works. The Calvinistic Methodists from the 1740s had their own periodicals, and subsequently, the better-known *Gospel Magazine*, while in the 1790s Alexander Kilham's followers ran the *Methodist Monitor*. In each case the brevity of the items allowed for short periods of concentration for busy working people, who could return repeatedly to the contents.

A religious magazine could be devoted to one theme. A newspaper, by contrast, needed to carry a variety of types of intelligence. Accordingly, eighteenth-century evangelicals tended not to found newspapers, although they showed considerable skill in arranging for material sympathetic to their cause to be inserted. Some newspaper proprietors, such as Felix Farley, whose *Bristol Journal* flourished in an area vital to early Methodism, were strong supporters of the Wesleys (Black 1987: 251, 256). This amounted to a skilful use of an existing medium rather than the invention of a new one. Evangelical publications tended not to encounter official censorship in the English-speaking world; the British Post Office facilitated, rather than obstructed, the circulation of newspapers in the second half of the eighteenth century (Ellis 1958: 55–9). The printed message was all the more important at a time, particularly before the defeat of Sidmouth's bill in 1811, when there were potential, and on occasions actual, difficulties over preaching, registration of meeting-houses and hostile mobs.

The Evangelical Revival both exploited and contributed to the development of print culture. It encouraged and in some cases provided encouragement for the acquisition of literacy. Admittedly, not all of those involved were committed evangelicals. Robert Raikes, of Sunday School fame, was also the owner of the *Gloucester Journal* (Black 1987: 256). But Gloucestershire was also the county of Hannah More (1745–1833), who combined popular education and philanthropy with the publication of brief and accessible religious tracts. That her works in the 1790s sold more than a million copies testifies to their low (and subsidized) price as well as a level of literacy which it would be unwise to underestimate. As an Anglican evangelical Hannah More, like Wesley, had well-connected friends, including Dr Johnson's circle; she subsequently became associated with John Newton, Wilberforce and the Clapham Sect. In the early years of the French Revolution she wrote a series of popular pamphlets, or essays, in which she deployed religious values in favour of the existing political system and against the challenge of the Jacobins at home and abroad. Using a semi-fictional style, with simple dialogues between easily recognizable stereotypes, she endeavoured to promote loyalty among the lower orders. Her *Cheap Repository Tracts* achieved enormous success, outstripping even that of Paine's *Rights of Man*, her principal target. Her message has been patronizingly, if engagingly, summarized as 'Burke for beginners'. The comparison is appropriate in that both drew on existing sources of strength – Burke on a corpus of Anglican political theory, More on a substantial and deep-rooted knowledge of the Bible which, although at times mediated through folk-religion and magical connotations, prepared the ground for her message.

That biblical awareness was deepened by the repetitive effect of psalms and hymns, a feature of the Revival which has perhaps received most attention of all. There is eloquent testimony to the power of psalm-singing to sustain the converted among the artisan families who contributed so much to the revival in western Scotland after 1740. The psalm helped to provide identification with the wider Revival for many humble individuals 'during lay-sponsored group activities such as religious societies, at home during family prayer, or while engaged in their increasingly solitary work at their looms or at their wheels' (Landsman 1989: 148). Biblical themes dominated the 5,000 or more of the hymns of Charles Wesley. Many other prominent evangelicals were authors of hymns which are still sung: Zinzendorf, Cennick, John Newton ('Amazing Grace'), Edward Perronet, Independent minister at Canterbury, ('All hail the power of Jesus' name!'). Newton's parish of Olney became synonymous with hymn-writing because of the presence of his friend and lay helper William Cowper (1731–1800), whose sad, insanity-ridden life was lightened not only by celebrated hymns ('God moves in a mysterious way'; 'Hark, my soul! It is the Lord') but by a sentimentalizing of small animals ('Epitaph for a hare'; 'The retired cat') which well reflected the cult of sensibility of the later eighteenth century and to which evangelicalism undoubtedly contributed.

While it is probably inappropriate to assume a wide gulf between the three, the memorizing and the regular singing of hymns could form a bridge between the literate, those with minimal literacy and the illiterate. So, too, did the female role in the Revival. Dr Field's research into Methodist membership lists has revealed that Methodism contained a higher proportion of women than did the population of England and Wales as a whole. The average proportion of 57.7 per cent female membership of Methodism was spread with remarkable consistency over the period 1759–1832 and over England, Scotland, Wales and Ireland (Field 1994: 158–9). The same author has also demonstrated that among the Baptist and Congregational churches between 1751 and 1825 the proportion of female membership was 58.6 per cent (Field 1993: 66). It was usually the woman of the house who first met the itinerant evangelical preacher and introduced the rest of the family both to the preacher and to the local meeting (Hempton 1996: 187). One of the earliest types of attack upon Methodism was based on the allegation that its preachers – including Wesley himself – were guilty of exploiting 'feminine weakness' and Bishop Lavington of Exeter was not the only critic to imply that there was more than religious affinity between some evangelical preachers and their female followers.

Its female members have been described as 'The tip of the iceberg of Methodism's oral culture' (Hempton 1996: 186). Their involvement in the print culture of Methodism was equally important. There is no doubt but that evangelical religion offered to women a series of roles unavailable elsewhere. It is of course true that the Catholic Church offered a career (and at times a necessary refuge) for women through its orders of nuns, though these were generally in decline during the eighteenth century. The Church of England, admittedly, placed women principally in the passive role of attender, recipient and member of an audience. Susannah Wesley, the mother of John and Charles, was highly untypical in the initiatives which she took in the place of an ineffectual curate at Epworth. The majority of Protestant clergymen in the eighteenth century were married; indeed, clerical celibacy was widely regarded as a 'popish' perversion. Wives and daughters, as well as mothers and sisters of clergymen could all play their auxiliary parts. Evangelical religion, however, created openings for more active roles for women. One of the most important was that of domestic visiting. To visit the sick and elderly, and to minister to the poor, did not violate conventional notions of gender division and was entirely consistent with the role of motherhood.

It might be suggested that a reason for the growth of female numbers within Methodism was the way in which it spoke the language of spiritual equality, particularly in the period before 1801. It is almost a truism that a religious revival, by reason of its very novelty and informality as well as suspicion on the part of the established order, relies upon (and has to rely upon) people from unconventional backgrounds. Examples in this period include the French prophetesses in early eighteenth-century London, the followers of the millenarian Joanna Southcott a century later and the Shakers in England and New York from the 1770s. Early Methodism, too, had a substantial number of female preachers, helpers and authors. Wesley, perhaps recalling his mother's influence and the employment of women by the Moravians at Herrnhut, was prepared to make exceptions to the injunctions against female preaching in the epistles of St Paul; there was a danger that otherwise, there might be defections to the Society of Friends, where no such prohibition was recognized (Chilcote 1991: 162–5). Such exceptions were also consistent with his stress upon experience, or 'experimental' religion. It was the very success of such preachers as Elizabeth Hurrell in Yorkshire and Lancashire, Sarah Crosby (who had been abandoned by her husband), Elizabeth Dickinson in Leeds, Ann Trip in the same town and Margaret Davidson, the first major Irish woman preacher, that made early Methodism seem to be disruptive of the social order. By their gender and, in many cases also by their youth, female preachers were seen as challenging fundamental male assumptions. But it might be that their presence contributed to the proportionately high level of female recruitment discussed above. The success of female class leadership was widely noted and almost certainly had the same effect.

Female preaching had been at its most widespread in the early days of the Revival, when religious meetings had an impromptu air and were conducted in the most informal of social settings, in the open air, and in buildings other than formally-constituted chapels. However, as Methodism and other evangelical groups developed a more rigid denominational structure in the nineteenth century, more traditional gender roles re-asserted themselves. From the 1790s one of the most successful Methodist preachers was Mary Barritt, who in 1802 married Zechariah Taft, the (subsequent) author of *Holy Women*, a vital source for the early female preacher. Her brand of evangelicalism, according to Chilcote, was 'no mere revivalism' of a temporary kind. She followed Wesley's example of organizing her followers in classes and retaining their loyalty. But after Wesley's death, she encountered increasing criticism from those who cited biblical sanction for an all-male priesthood. The Dublin conference of Irish Methodism in 1802 resolved to prohibit women from preaching in public and to deny a membership ticket to any woman who defied that injunction (Chilcote 1991: 228–33). A similar prohibition was passed by the Methodist Conference in England, meeting at Manchester, the following year. Among Methodist break-away groups, including the New Connexion, female preaching was countenanced for much longer. Among the Bible Christian Methodists of Devon and Cornwall, women preachers flourished; 27 of them were publicly named in their circuit lists in 1825–7, although only one of them was still active in 1863 (Murray 1995: 101). Gradually, however, female preaching (extensive in Britain and North America, perhaps less so in Ireland) declined in relative importance.

Attempts were also made to restrict other aspects of the female role within evangelicalism. During the early years of the *Arminian Magazine*, under John Wesley's editorship, it was quite common for women to write of their own inner spiritual experiences and to describe their own lives. Although a measure of editing and conforming to what was expected and acceptable cannot be overlooked, there was a measure of personal autonomy in this female writing and at times there were oblique mentions of female preaching. But in the early nineteenth century, when the magazine was edited by the stern opponent of female participation Joseph Benson, that sense of autonomy faded and women tended to be relegated to the role of noble helpmeets to male preachers.

The female commitment to evangelicalism none the less continued to be a considerable one. There was still scope for the female hymn writer and poet, of whom Anne Dutton is an outstanding example. The *Evangelical Magazine* frequently reviewed work by female poets. Above all, the host of voluntary societies spawned by the movement provided numerous outlets for female abilities. 'Through evangelicalism, persuasion became a way of life for thousands of women in nineteenth-century Ireland' (Hempton 1996: 189); the Ladies Society of the London Hibernian Society, for instance, ran 190 schools with 8,000 scholars in 1830. In early nineteenth-century America, evangelicalism promoted the involvement of women in many political campaigns, particularly of a philanthropic, but sometimes of a party political, kind. Antislavery drew women into campaigns for the ante-bellum Republican party on a large scale, despite their exclusion from the franchise and in obvious defiance of conventional notions defining 'separate spheres' (Carwardine 1993: 31–5). In Britain the female involvement in class and band leadership, in taking the initiative in charitable work, was not retarded. Much value was attached to the example which could be set by female piety and women were often at the forefront of mid-nineteenth century prayer meetings for revival. The marginalization of women has, possibly, been exaggerated. In a fascinating survey, *Family Fortunes*, Davidoff and Hall conclude that 'modern' class and gender relations underwent their formative period between 1780 and 1850 and that evangelical religion helped to create a new moral climate in which a distinctive middle class could flourish. A consequence was that patriarchal stereotypes were reinforced and that certain 'public' spaces – theatres, pleasure gardens, assembly rooms – became less available to women. But the association of evangelicalism with the middle classes and the confining of women to a domestic sphere are both open to question. We have seen that a high proportion of Methodist adherents were skilled artisans and tradesmen, with more than a sprinkling of the labouring classes. The aristocratic and gentry involvement in evangelical endeavour, though very much a minority affair, cannot be ignored either. Moreover, the post-French Revolution period witnessed a good deal of female participation in the various activities of patriotic associations and Dr Vickery may well be correct in suggesting that the public assertion of a doctrine of 'separate spheres' in the nineteenth century, far from reflecting reality, amounted to a wistful aspiration (Vickery 1993: 400).

This discussion of the wider ripples of evangelicalism has so far concentrated mainly upon nonconformity. But of course, even after the departure of Methodism from its ranks, the Church of England still retained the loyalty of many men and women who shared evangelical values. It was suggested by Halévy that such people formed a kind of 'rearguard' within the Church to maintain another front in the evangelical advance; and by Ford K. Brown in *Fathers of the Victorians* that they were seeking to take power in Church and state. Both propositions need to be viewed with some scepticism. We have seen that many of the earliest evangelical conversions in the eighteenth century took place among Anglican clergymen who had no contact with the leaders of Methodism. Similarly, in the early nineteenth century, the ability of Anglican Evangelicals to co-operate with their Nonconformist counterparts in areas of mutual agreement, for instance in the (officially) non-denominational London Missionary Society, hardly implied a deeper alliance to subvert the Church from within. Within the Church, too, it would be more appropriate to speak of the promotion of certain evangelical values rather than the launching of a bid for power. In parts of the country, groups of Evangelical clergymen drew each other into informal 'circles' to promote their ideals and to succour each others' pastoral work. Somerset, strategically placed between two of the most important early centres of the Revival – Bristol and Cornwall – was home to at least 19 such clergy in the last third of the eighteenth century (Gibson 1986: 135). Of course, positions of influence were advantageous in the promotion of such values, but there were many clergymen sympathetic to them who would not have called themselves, or been labelled by others, as evangelical. Beilby Porteus, Bishop of London from 1787 to 1808, was a strong critic of the slave trade, an advocate of missions to the Caribbean and a campaigner for sabbath observance and a stricter enforcement of public morals. Yet the first Evangelical to be appointed to an English bishopric is usually reckoned to have been Henry Ryder, who became Bishop of Gloucester in 1815. Even he probably owed his appointment more to family connection than to his theological opinions; two of his brothers served in the cabinet. Shades of opinion were often too blurred for the sort of precise labelling into 'parties' that the theses mentioned above seem to demand.

There can be no doubt, however, as to the growth of evangelicalism within the Church itself from the final quarter of the eighteenth century. Among the clergy the universities remained the essential training-grounds. At Oxford, the relatively unfashionable St Edmund Hall, whence Calvinistic Methodists had been expelled for non-attendance at chapel in 1768, became an Evangelical stronghold, particularly under its energetic vice-principal Isaac Crouch. The familiar pattern of the support-group emerged at the Hall, with regular Sunday evening reading parties and a dining club. The importance of Crouch's work lay in the fact that, as Dr Reynolds puts it, 'the type of man commonly produced at St Edmund Hall went quietly to work in his parish, and thereby became an important if inconspicuous part of the backbone of the evangelical movement and the anglican system' (Reynolds 1975: 63). One of Crouch's pupils, the Rev. Joseph Mendham, became curate to John Riland at Sutton Coldfield; Riland had been assistant to Henry Venn at Huddersfield in the

1770s, and so an evangelical 'line of succession' was formed. Mendham became a leading polemicist against Catholicism in the 1830s and 1840s. Cambridge University, too, sent many of its graduates out as parish priests and they too numbered many Evangelicals. In the university a key figure was Charles Simeon (1759–1836), a Fellow of King's College and from 1783 until his death vicar of Holy Trinity Church in the city. His influence upon generations of undergraduates was considerable and he consolidated it by founding the 'Simeon Trustees' to acquire ecclesiastical patronage. At the same time, the changing theological climate of the university was symbolized by Isaac Milner's election as president of Queens' College in 1788 (and for the statutory two-year term as vice-chancellor in 1792). Milner was not only a committed evangelical but a stern opponent of the kind of antitrinitarian heterodoxy which had flourished in the university in the preceding decades. It was largely through his influence that the Unitarian sympathizer and political radical William Frend was tried before the vice-chancellor's court and dismissed from the university in 1793. The theological tone of the Anglican Evangelicals tended towards a moderate Calvinism which distinguished them from the Arminianism of the Wesleyan Methodists but which did not have the chilling effect of the more rigorously predestinarian 'hyper' or 'high' Calvinism. Simeon, for instance, held both to a form of predestination and of free-will, since scripture could be said to sanction both, and such an apparent contradiction had, in the last resort, to be ascribed to divine inscrutability.

The most effective pursuit of evangelical values in public life, however, may be attributed to Anglican laymen and women. Hannah More, though exceptional, was not unique as a female religious author. Nor was she unique in belonging to a cluster of like-minded Evangelicals, of which the best-known was the Clapham sect. Its rector, John Venn, the son of the more famous vicar of Huddersfield, was a member of one of the most famous Evangelical clerical dynasties. The Clapham sect included William Wilberforce (1759–1833), for forty-five years the most important Evangelical in Parliament (as MP firstly for Hull, then, from 1784 for the country's largest constituency, Yorkshire). He exerted more influence in promoting Evangelical values even than Spencer

Percival, the 'Evangelical prime minister' (from 1809 until his assassination in 1812), who shared Wilberforce's anti-slavery convictions, his concern for public morals (he wished to make adultery a criminal offence) and for family prayers.

The values by which Evangelicals were becoming known may briefly be summarized under the headings of political, humanitarian and moral. In terms of party politics in the nineteenth century, Evangelicals tended to be associated (not always accurately) with Toryism and one reason for that was that they were more interested in personal, moral reformation than in the reform of the constitution or a broadening of the political nation in a 'democratic' direction. Wilberforce, for example, in the 1780s consistently supported efforts in Parliament to curb election expenses and the attendant opportunities for corruption; he considered that to be more important than the franchise. He was also a supporter of economical reform and the opening of government accounts to a greater degree of public scrutiny. He was far from alone in this view. Lord North and the Younger Pitt, neither of whom may be regarded as Evangelicals, did more than any other politicians to facilitate that process, and there were non-evangelical arguments in its favour, notably the need for greater public efficiency after the disasters of the War of American Independence. But personal accountability to God for the disposal of one's time and income could easily translate itself into a demand for a similar accountability in the public sphere. It may be found at exceptionally high levels in the diaries of W.E. Gladstone (born 1809), whose early life was passed under the strongest evangelical influences.

It would be inappropriate to suggest that evangelicals possessed a monopoly of righteousness (or self-righteousness) or that they were unique in seeking to apply Christian values to public life. The attack upon the slave trade and upon slavery itself fully bears this out. Anti-slavery exerted a unifying effect across and within denominational and religious boundaries. It was a cause in which not only Arminian and Calvinist, but evangelical and Unitarian could co-operate. By 1800, British abolitionism had drawn together many diverse elements, with varying reasons for seeking the end of the slave trade. The specifically evangelical contribution, in Roger Anstey's view, was to apply to a political issue the theological values of Arminianism: salvation open to all, redemption, benevolence and the role of providence and to translate those values from the personal to the parliamentary and imperial spheres (Anstey 1975: 184–99). Professor Anstey makes full allowance for the (much earlier) Quaker involvement and for the different motives of those whose interest in the subject was dictated by more secular considerations. But the rise of popular abolitionist sentiment in late eighteenth-century Britain at the same time as evangelical values were entering, if not dominating, public life was no coincidence. Thomas Clarkson, by campaigning in the country and greatly enhancing the status of the lecture as a means of public information, and William Wilberforce, by campaigning in the House of Commons, ensured victory for the abolitionists in the moral argument. By the 1790s they had reduced the defence of the trade to reasons of economic necessity. Anstey is also careful to demolish any myth that the abolition of the British slave trade in 1806–7, and the successful resistance to any attempt to renew it thereafter, was the result of unqualified altruism. National self-interest, in the form of a reluctance to sanction the supply of slaves to newly-captured territories which might be returned to the French at the peace treaty, also played a part. However, the evangelical achievement lay partly in the mobilization of a popular petitioning campaign which eclipsed contemporary political causes (notably parliamentary reform) by its sheer weight of numbers. In its appeal to elements outside the elite, including women, evangelicalism was not exactly conforming to the conservative, even reactionary, image constructed by its opponents. Without doubt, evangelicalism contributed to the popularity of anti-slavery; and this association with what became the best-supported political cause of the entire period worked to the ultimate benefit of evangelicalism.

To evangelicals, anti-slavery became a divinely-ordained duty in which those to be liberated were to be brought to the knowledge of the gospel. Others, including Unitarians, Whigs and political radicals, conceived anti-slavery much more in terms of human rights and inalienable civil liberties. Yet while evangelical religion did not pose a direct challenge to crown or constitution, or to the existing structure of property relationships, in Britain, by taking up humanitarian issues it was capable of stimulating a mild political radicalism. Silas Told was one of many who ministered to condemned prisoners. Like Wesley in his attitudes towards the poor, Told was no mere apologist for a static society. In the northern United States, evangelicalism across a range of Protestant denominations was a crucial element which helped to create the Republican party as a radical, anti-slavery coalition in the 1850s, in which emancipation of the slaves overrode considerations of property. Campaigning for John C. Frémont, the Republican candidate in the presidential election of 1865, was equated with gospel preaching and revivalism. One religious newspaper called the election a 'great awakening', to be 'classified among the moral reformations of the world' (quoted in Carwardine 1993: 269). Some southern evangelicals formulated a Christian, biblically-based defence of slavery in the 1840s and 1850s and Carwardine sees the split between northern and southern evangelicalism as the fundamental cause of the Civil War, a conflict which could not, in his judgement, have been initiated solely by 'concern over economic interests' (Carwardine 1993: 322–3).

The moral reforming priorities of evangelicals in some ways reveal their late seventeenth-century High Church origins. In June 1787 a Royal Proclamation against Vice and Immorality gave rise to the Proclamation Society (replaced in 1802 by the better-known Society for the Suppression of Vice). It had the support of the king, some bishops and other members of the elite, but was very largely the work of Wilberforce. He had studied Woodward's *History of the Society for the Reformation of Manners in the year 1692* for this purpose. His celebrated diary entry in 1787, 'God Almighty has set before me two great objects, the suppression of the slave trade and the reformation of manners' (quoted in Walvin 1980: 149) owed the second of those objects to the example of the late seventeenth century. The Proclamation Society and its successors were in large part responsible for exposing evangelicalism to one of its severest criticisms, namely that it sought to impose upper and middle class notions of respectability upon the less fortunate. The Whig clergyman Sydney Smith shrewdly observed that the Society for the Suppression of Vice was interested only in the suppression of the vices of those with incomes of under five hundred pounds per annum; bear-baiting was to be outlawed, but hunting, the pastime of the wealthy, was not. Smith, admittedly, was strongly prejudiced against all things evangelical, but there

was some force in his strictures. For the poor, a sense of inter-
ference with traditional pleasures was a more obvious evangelical
characteristic than the strong attacks often launched by evangelicals upon the luxury, extravagance and irreligion of the rich,
attacks exemplified in Wilberforce's *Practical View of the prevailing religious system of professed Christians in the higher and
middle classes in this country contrasted with real Christianity*
(1797) and imitated by numerous lesser writers.

There was one aspect of evangelicalism which harmonized well
with much plebeian, as well as elite, opinion. This was anti-Catholicism. We have seen how fear of Catholic advance upon Protestant minorities and states was a contributory factor in the early
years of the continental revival. In later periods, evangelicalism
did not lose its detestation of Rome; indeed, in the early nineteenth century that detestation intensified. With the move towards
the centre of the political stage of Catholic Emancipation in
Britain and Ireland, horror stories about Catholic intolerance and
persecution were revived. As Catholics began to enter public life;
as Catholic voters in Ireland could (after 1829) return MPs of their
own faith to the Union Parliament at Westminster and as Irish
immigration into Britain gave rise to competition in the housing
and employment markets, sectarian feeling, far from dormant in
the eighteenth century, flared up again. The state had amended
the constitution to remove most of the anti-Catholic stipulations
of 1688–9 and into the vacuum sprang a raw, popular 'ultra' Protestantism which saw Catholic Emancipation as a fundamental
betrayal. Some of the most vehement anti-Catholic agitators in
mid-nineteenth century Britain were Protestant Irish missionaries,
such as William Murphy. Methodist membership in Ireland had
indeed grown to 36,903 by 1830, although by that time its rate of
expansion had slowed considerably (Hempton 1996: 36); but in a
total Irish population of 7.7 million this was a figure small enough
to emphasize both the limitations of the Revival as far as the
Catholic majority was concerned and the continuing sense of Protestant unease at any prospect of Irish home rule. In the 1830s and
1840s there was a type of Tory opinion which hoped to reverse
Catholic Emancipation as well as to prevent any further Catholic
advance; it had much evangelical support in the country as a
whole and played some part in the Tory victory in the general

111

election of 1841. At the popular level it found a voice in such periodicals as *The Record*; at a more intellectual level it found expression in such works as Joseph Mendham's study of the Council of Trent and in such bodies as the Reformation Society (1827) and the Evangelical Alliance (1845–6). In the United States there were equivalent organizations, notably the American Protestant Society (1844) and the American and Foreign Christian Union (1849) (Wolffe 1994: 179–93). That some evangelical groups regarded themselves as the repositories of the Protestant tradition was a legacy of the revival which lasted into the twentieth century. It helps to explain the late entry of Catholics to the highest offices in Britain and the fact that the United States did not elect a Catholic president until 1960.

This is evidence that the 'ecumenical' instincts within evangelicalism amounted to an eirenicism within, rather than beyond, the Protestant world. It is also an indication that evangelicalism retained popular – or populist – Protestant instincts at a time when much respectable opinion, at least in Parliament, was shedding its older anti-Catholic attitudes. The middle class respectability with which evangelicalism is so often associated sat uneasily with the raucousness and violence of the anti-Catholic mob. To study evangelical anti-Catholicism is to encounter a corrective to some of the more self-congratulatory accounts of the revival which claim that its wider effects were almost wholly favourable. The Evangelical Revival left a complex and ambiguous legacy both in terms of its theological and ethical values.

# Conclusion

Although the climacteric years of the Evangelical Revival may reasonably be said to have ended by the 1830s, it would be mistaken to suppose that the phenomenon of the religious revival ceased to appear. The change in the post-1830 age involved a certain lack of spontaneity. The revivals examined in this book were often characterized by their unpredictable and apparently impromptu nature, which caused such astonishment to contemporaries. Thereafter, there were numerous revivals, mainly of a local nature, but they were much more likely to be planned in advance. As Dr Bebbington comments, 'spontaneity gradually gave way to arranged revivals' (Bebbington 1989: 116). Whereas in the early eighteenth century, mass conversions had led to the use of the term 'revival', from the early nineteenth century it was much more likely that a revival would be deliberately induced, in the hope of gaining conversions. Even before 1800 in the Methodist stronghold of Cornwall, Dr Luker has shown that the activation of revival was conscious policy and was part of a cyclical process involving fluctuations in membership in which a period of unusual enthusiasm within the Church itself led to revivalist preaching which led to an increase in recruitment which proved to be only temporary (Luker 1986: 607–11). One reason for the more stereotyped and formulaic type of revival was the growth of a body of literature which took a somewhat prescriptive line, offering advice as to how revivals should be conducted. An important example was *Lectures on Revivals in Religion*, by Charles Finney, published in 1835 in America and four years later in Britain.

As preparation for revivals became more systematic, and was

often aimed at specific groups in a community or congregation, the term itself came to acquire a more precise meaning. The Evangelical Revival of the years 1700–1830 was really a series of separate, though connected, revivals, some of them of a very brief character. Similarly, a revival in the nineteenth century was often a local affair, preceded by services and prayer meetings to create a sense of expectation and reaching a climax with a well-publicized visit from a celebrated preacher (Carwardine 1978: 78–9). There was a difference, however, between the kind of revival which could enthuse a small village for a short period and leave no lasting impression, and that which could inspire imitation elsewhere and secure its place in history by bequeathing a body of written evidence. There was also a considerable difference between a revival which could enthuse a small village in a wave of excitement for a few years, and an 'awakening', which could exert longer-term effects in a truly continental dimension. It has been appropriate for the purposes of this book to use the word 'Revival' with a capital R as an 'umbrella' term to signify many local revivals, and several broader 'awakenings', on a world-wide scale.

Much 'revival' literature emerged from groups outside the religious establishment. Although the early phases of the Revival internationally owed much to established churches, the main impetus in the nineteenth century was to be found outside those churches. The American constitution, by forbidding the establishment of a federal church, contributed to the religious pluralism in which popular evangelicalism could thrive. A free religious market was one which favoured the individualistic accents of evangelicalism. Hence it has been suggested that a major long-term contribution of Wesleyan Methodism to British society was a considerable stimulus to individual liberty, laissez-faire and free trade – the classic values of Victorian liberalism. The clearest statement of this thesis is to be found in Bernard Semmel's *The Methodist Revolution* (1974). A key aspect of it hinges upon the relationship which is claimed between Wesleyan Arminianism and individual responsibility in economic and social life. There is a hint of irony here, however, in that Wesleyans inclined towards Toryism during the later nineteenth century; there is evidence that many of them deserted the Liberal party over home rule in the

1880s, while most other nonconformists retained their traditional allegiance. Moreover if Arminianism was the key, the thesis will hardly work for Calvinist evangelicals (or Evangelicals). However, an association between evangelicalism and liberal politics is by no means wholly fanciful.

Some evangelical campaigns against sin were bound to be unpopular with the public, especially if they involved attacks on popular pleasures. Others, however, by provoking conflict with vested interests, were more equivocal. The temperance movement of the nineteenth century, in which evangelicals were heavily concerned, fell into both categories. Although restrictions on hours of drink would always encounter popular objections, evangelicals also found themselves arrayed against the brewing industry; the Liberal ministry's Licensing Act of 1872 helped to push the brewing interest into the ranks of the Conservatives. Bands of Hope and Temperance Societies, often demanding total prohibition, owed much to evangelical initiative. It is notable that many leading figures in the early Labour movement acquired their first, essential, speaking experience on the platforms of Temperance Leagues. Keir Hardie is a good example; Arthur Henderson had been a Wesleyan preacher. It is true that recent research into the social composition of Methodist membership has shown that that vital branch of evangelicalism did not exert its strongest appeal to the very poor. But it succeeded in conveying an impression of a critical attitude towards some elements of private enterprise far enough to justify the aphorism that the Labour party owed more to Methodism than to Marx. Certainly the appeal of evangelicalism beyond the elite helps to explain why most political radicalism in Britain did not take the extreme anti-clerical (or anti-religious) form which it did take in late nineteenth-century France, Italy and Spain.

A final comment concerns the world of missions. Some of the earliest heroes of evangelicalism were overseas missionaries of the type of Henry Martyn (1781–1812), a colleague of Simeon in Cambridge, a chaplain for the East India Company and a plausible prototype for St John Rivers of *Jane Eyre*. The export of evangelical Christianity beyond Europe and North America could be interpreted as the fulfilment of prophecy and a host of nineteenth-century hymns gloried in the expansion of missionary work. The element of 'cultural imperialism', the sense of superiority which gave rise to such lines as 'The heathen in his blindness/bows down to wood and stone', cannot, of course, be overlooked; nor can the attachment to empire, as the provider of opportunities for religious mission, on the part of some evangelicals. General Gordon and David Livingstone both owed much to this ethos. The legacy of evangelicalism in its worldwide sense, however, did more than merely cement the hegemony of the European overseas empires. In colonial societies, evangelical missionaries were not always perceived as agents of the imperial exploiter. Indeed, missionaries were often among the sternest critics of traders and settlers. This is demonstrated by the success of evangelical churches in former colonies. The Moravian Church provides a striking example. As we have seen, the eighteenth-century Moravians did not seek to found a new church and, indeed, made efforts not to do so. But at the end of the twentieth century they remain a significant world force. In 1995, the total membership of the Moravian Church was 764,852; of these, 364,581 were citizens of the four provinces of Tanzania. This compares with a membership of 4,090 in Britain and 50,223 in the United States (*Moravian Almanac* 1997: 7). Some of the most telling evidence as to the continuing appeal of the Revival internationally is to be found in the Third World, in Korea and in the Pentecostal movement in Latin America.

Missions were partly responsible for the cult of the physically robust, temperate, ascetic and self-sacrificing individual who would characteristically ascribe good health to sobriety and religious self-discipline. There could have been no finer exemplar than John Wesley himself, who lived into his eighty-eighth year, despite an (initially) delicate constitution, through just such a regime. It was an ideal pursued at the Countess of Huntingdon's college at Cheshunt, the successor to Trevecca, where the students were expected to rise at five in the morning and endure a day of the most rigorous study (quarter of an hour for breakfast, half an hour for dinner, quarter of an hour for supper). At mealtimes, 'One of the students or probationers, by rotation, must read a Chapter in the Bible, which will prevent unprofitable conversation and afford matter for meditation' (Welch 1990: 167). One may, perhaps, concede, that in this case ambitions possibly outran realities, and that Cheshunt College sought to impose impossible standards of self-denial. But in the Cheshunt regulations there is none the less evident the demand for personal austerity and, by direct implication, the purging from public life of luxury and corruption, which was to be a hallmark of evangelicalism. The evangelical voice as critic of self-indulgence is likely to be heard in any age and it is not a voice which will always be unequivocally on the side of the secular powers. The ethical values of the Evangelical Revival were derived from and justified by theology. It is likely, however, that those ethical values will be its most enduring memorial.

# Glossary

| | |
|---|---|
| ANTINOMIANISM | The belief that those chosen by God for salvation are exempt from the need to observe any moral law; strongly denounced by John Wesley and attributed by him to some of his Calvinist opponents. |
| ARIANISM | A belief, originating in the fourth century AD, which was critical of the doctrine of the Trinity and regarded Christ as subordinate to God the Father, to whom alone worship should be offered. |
| ARMINIANISM | The belief that the death of Christ was an atoning sacrifice for all humanity, not solely for the elect who had been predestined by God for salvation. It insisted on the human will to accept or reject the offer of salvation. |
| CALVINISM | The beliefs associated with John Calvin (1509–64), of which the most important from the point of view of this book was the conviction that some persons (the elect) were pre-destined to salvation and the non-elect to damnation. |
| COVENANTER | The radical Presbyterians of seventeenth-century Scotland who waged |

an ultimately successful campaign against the episcopal Church, which was associated with the Stuart monarchy.

DEISM
The view that the evidence for the existence of God may be appreciated by human reason in the harmonious ordering of the universe. Deists regarded God as the creator of the universe who thereafter withdrew from active intervention in its affairs. They played down the authority of the Bible.

JUSTIFICATION
The means by which God pardons human sins and treats sinners who repent and have due faith as if they were righteous. It does not amount to redemption, which delivers humanity from sin and brings former sinners back into communion with God.

LATITUDINARIANISM
A way of thought in the late seventeenth and eighteenth-century Church of England which, though orthodox on most theological points, played down doctrinal differences and advocated acceptance of diverse opinions within the Church and toleration for Protestant Dissenters outside it.

MILLENARIANISM
The belief in a second coming of Christ. Pre-millennialists believed that the millennium, the reign of Christ on earth for a thousand years, would follow the second coming; post-millennialists believed that it would precede the millennium and prepare the way for it.

NON-JUROR
Members of the Church of England who were unable, on grounds of conscience, to take the oaths of allegiance to the regime of William and Mary

after 1688. Several hundred clergy were deprived of their appointments for this reason; they contributed an important element to eighteenth-century religious thought.

ORIGINAL SIN The belief that all humanity is born into sin following the Fall of Adam and therefore is in need of redemption through the atoning death of Christ.

RANTERS A term applied to religious radicals, many of them antinomians, of the period of the Interregnum (1649–60). It was sometimes used abusively of preachers of the Evangelical Revival.

SOCINIANISM A more extreme form of Arianism, whereby the divinity of Christ is denied and he is regarded as a divinely-inspired human being. Socinians denied that the death of Christ was an atonement for human sins. In the eighteenth century the term Unitarian was generally applied to the holders of this belief.

TROPUS The idea, associated mainly with Count Zinzendorf, which saw each Church as a tropus, or 'school of wisdom', as a move towards a greater (Protestant) Christian unity. He had hoped that his Moravian followers in England would become an 'Anglican tropus' within the established Church. Instead, the Act of 1749 recognized them as a separate entity.

# Select bibliography

## 1. MANUSCRIPT SOURCES
British Library:
Additional Manuscript 32973 (Newcastle Papers)
Additional Manuscript 59307 (Grenville Papers)

## 2. CONTEMPORARY PERIODICALS
*Arminian Magazine*
*Evangelical Magazine*
*Gentleman's Magazine*
*London Journal*
*Methodist Magazine*

## 3. CONTEMPORARY WORKS AND WORKS INCORPORATING CONTEMPORARY SOURCES

*These entries are listed in alphabetical order of the contemporary source.*

Bronte, C. *Jane Eyre* [eds. J. Jack & M. Smith] (Oxford: Clarendon Press, 1969).

Ward, W.R. *The early correspondence of Jabez Bunting.* Camden Society fourth series, Volume 11 (London: Royal Historical Society, 1972).

Cooper, J.H. (ed.) *Extracts from the Journals of John Cennick: Moravian Evangelist.* (Glengormley: Moravian History Magazine, 1996).

Welch, E. (ed.) *Cheshunt College: the early years. A selections of records* (Hertford: Hertfordshire Record Society, 1990).

Goen, C.G. (ed.) *The Works of Jonathan Edwards* Vol.4 (New Haven and London: Yale University Press, 1972).

Boynton, L. Oxford in 1742: A letter of the Revd John Gambold. *History of Universities* **XIII**, 301–12, 1994.

Brewer, S. (ed.) *The Early Letters of Bishop Richard Hurd 1739–1762* Vol. 3 (Woodbridge: Church of England Record Society, 1995).

Johnson, S. 1755/photographic reprint *A Dictionary of the English language* (Harlow: Longman, 1990).

Elwin, M. *The Noels and the Milbankes. Their letters for twenty five years, 1767–1792* (London: Macdonald, 1967).

Toon, P. (ed.) *The Life, walk and triumph of faith. By William Romaine.* With an account of his life and work by Peter Toon (Cambridge: James Clarke, 1970).

Scott, T. *The Force of truth: an authentic narrative*, 3rd edn (London: C. Watts, 1790).

Knapp, L.M. (ed.) *The Letters of Tobias Smollett* (Oxford: Clarendon Press, 1970).

Stockdale, J. *Parliamentary Register* [for 1774–1780] [17 volumes] (London: Stockdale, 1775–80).

Taft, Z. 1825/8 *Biographical sketches of the lives of various holy women* (London: Methodist Publishing House, 1992).

Told, S. *The Life of Mr Silas Told written by himself. With a Note to the Serious and Candid Reader by John Wesley, A.M.* (London: Epworth Press [first published 1786], 1954).

Venn, H. (ed.) *The Life and a selection from the letters of the late Rev. Henry Venn* (London: John Hatchard, 1834).

Lewis, W.S. *Horace Walpole's Correspondence* [48 volumes] (London & New Haven: Oxford University Press/Yale University Press, 1937–83).

Heitzenrater, R.P. *et al.* (eds) *The Bicentennial Edition of the Works of John Wesley.* 27 volumes to date, 1970– (Oxford: Oxford University Press and Nashville: Abingdon Press (cited as 'Wesley'), 1970).

Whitefield, G. *Letters of George Whitefield. For the period 1734–1742* (London: Banner of Truth Trust, 1771/1976).

Whitehead, J. *A discourse delivered at the New Chapel in the City-Road, on the ninth of March 1791, at the funeral of the late Rev. Mr John Wesley* (London, 1791).

Woodforde, J. In *The diary of a country parson. The Reverend James Woodforde*, Beresford, J. (ed.) (Oxford: Clarendon Press, 1924–31).

Beresford, J. (ed.) *The diary of a country parson. The Reverend James Woodforde* [5 volumes] (Oxford: Clarendon Press, 1924–31).

Gibson, D. (ed.) *A Parson in the Vale of White Horse. George Woodward's letters from East Hendred, 1753–1761* (Gloucester: Alan Sutton, 1982).

Betham-Edwards, M. (ed.) *The Autobiography of Arthur Young with selections from his correspondence* (London: Smith Elder, 1898).

4. SECONDARY SOURCES

Addison, W.G. *The renewed Church of the United Brethren 1722-1930* (London: SPCK, 1932).

*Anglican–Moravian Conversations. The Fetter Lane Common Statement. With essays in Anglican and Moravian History by Colin Podmore.* (Melksham, Wiltshire: Council for Christian Unity of the General Synod of the Church of England, Occasional Paper No. 5, 1996).

Anstey, R.T. *The Atlantic Slave Trade and British Abolition 1760–1810* (London and Basingstoke: Macmillan, 1975).

Armstrong, A. *The Church of England, the Methodists and Society 1700–1850* (London: University of London Press Ltd, 1973).

Baker, F. The early experiences of Fletcher of Madeley. *Proceedings of the Wesley Historical Society*, **XXXIII**, 25–9, 1961.

Baker, F. *John Wesley and the Church of England* (London: Epworth, 1970).

Baskerville, S.W. 'The Political behaviour of the Cheshire clergy, 1705–1752'. *Northern History* **XXIII**, 74–97, 1987.

Bebbington, D.W. *Evangelicalism in Modern Britain. A History from the 1730s to the 1980s* (London: Unwin Hyman, 1989).

Black, J. *The English Press in the Eighteenth Century* (Edinburgh: Donald, 1987).

Black, J. *Eighteenth Century Europe 1700–1789* (London: Macmillan, 1990).

Bolam, C.G., J. Goring, H.L. Short, R. Thomas *The English Presbyterians. From Elizabethan Puritanism to Modern Unitarianism* (London: Allen & Unwin, 1968).

Bradley, I. *The Call to seriousness. The Evangelical impact on the Victorians* (London: Jonathan Cape, 1976).

Brown, C.G. *The Social History of Religion in Scotland since 1730* (London: Methuen, 1987).

Brown, F.K. *Fathers of the Victorians. The Age of Wilberforce* (Cambridge: Cambridge University Press, 1961).

Brown, S.J. *Thomas Chalmers and the Godly Commonwealth in Scotland* (Oxford: Oxford University Press, 1982).

Butler, D. *Methodists and Papists. John Wesley and the Catholic Church in the eighteenth century* (London: Darton, Longman and Todd, 1995).

Carwardine, R. *Trans-Atlantic Revivalism. Popular Evangelicalism in Britain and America, 1790–1865* (Westport, Conn: Greenwood Press, 1978).

Carwardine, R.J. *Evangelicals and Politics in Antebellum America* (New Haven and London: Yale University Press, 1993).

Chilcote, P.W. *John Wesley and the women preachers of early Methodism* (Metachen, N.J. & London: American Theological Library Association and Scarecrow Press, 1991).

Christie, I.R. *Stress and stability in late eighteenth-century Britain. Reflections on the British avoidance of Revolution* (Oxford: Clarendon Press, 1984).

Clark, J.C.D. *English Society 1688–1832. Ideology, social structure and political practice during the* ancien régime (Cambridge: Cambridge University Press, 1985).

Clifford, A.C. *Authentic Calvinism. A clarification* (Norwich: Chareton Reformed Publishing, 1996).

Colley, L. *Britons. Forging the Nation 1707-1837* (New Haven and London: Yale University Press, 1992).

Cross, F.L. and Livingstone, E.A. (ed.) *Oxford Dictionary of the Christian Church* (London: Oxford University Press, 1974).

Crawford, M.J. 'Origins of the eighteenth-century Evangelical Revival: England and New England compared'. *Journal of British Studies*, 26(4), 361–97, 1987.

Crawford, M.J. *Seasons of Grace. Colonial New England's Revival tradition in its British context* (Oxford: Oxford University Press, 1991).

Currie, R., A. Gilbert, L. Horsley *Churches and churchgoers. Patterns of church growth in the British Isles since 1700* (Oxford: Clarendon Press, 1977).

Davidoff, L. & C. Hall *Family Fortunes. Men and women of the English middle class, 1780–1850* (London: Routledge, 1992).

Davie, D. *A Gathered Church. The Literature of the English Dissenting Interest, 1700–1930* (London and Henley: Routledge & Kegan Paul, 1978).

Davies, O. 'Methodism, the clergy and the popular belief in witchcraft and magic'. *History* 82, 252–65, 1997.

Davis, R.W. *Dissent in Politics 1780–1830. The Political Life of William Smith M.P.* (London: Epworth Press, 1971).

Ellis, K.L. *The Post Office in the Eighteenth Century* (London: Oxford University Press, 1958).

Evans, E.J. 'The Anglican Clergy of Northern England'. (See C. Jones (ed.), 221–40, 1987).

Fawcett, A. *The Cambuslang Revival. The Scottish Evangelical Revival of the Eighteenth Century* (London: Banner of Truth Trust, 1971).

Ferguson, J. *The Religious Revival in England* (Bletchley: Open University Press, 1972).

Field, C.D. (ed.) *John Fletcher, 1729–1785: A Methodist bicentenary* (Manchester: John Rylands University Library of Manchester, 1985).

Field, C.D. 'Adam and Eve: gender in the English Free Church constituency'. *Journal of Ecclesiastical History* 44(1), 63–79, 1993.

Field, C.D. 'The social composition of English Methodism to 1830: a membership analysis'. *Bulletin of the John Rylands University Library of Manchester* 76(1), 153–69, 1994.

Geyer-Kordesch, J. 'Halle, University of'. In *A Dictionary of eighteenth-century world history*, J. Black & R. Porter (eds), 311–2 (Oxford: Blackwell, 1994).

Gibson, W. 'Somerset Evangelical Clergy'. *Somerset Archaeology and Natural History*, 130, 135–40, 1986.

Gibson, W. *Church, State and Society, 1760–1850* (London: Macmillan, 1994).

Gilbert, A.D. *Religion and society in industrial England. Church, Chapel and social change, 1740–1914* (London: Longman, 1976).

Gilbert, A.D. 'Methodism, Dissent and political stability in early industrial England'. *Journal of Religious History* 10(4), 381–99, 1979.

Gilbert, A.D. 'Religion and political stability in early industrial England'. In *The Industrial Revolution and British society*, P.K. O'Brien & R. Quinault (eds), 79–99 (Cambridge: Cambridge University Press, 1993).

Gregory, J. 'The eighteenth-century Reformation: the pastoral task of Anglican clergy after 1689'. (See Walsh, Haydon & Taylor, 67–85, 1993).

Halévy, E. *A History of the English People in the nineteenth century. I. England in 1815* (London: Benn, 1913/1960).

Hamilton, J.T. & K.G. Hamilton *History of the Moravian Church. The Renewed Unitas Fratrum 1722–1957* (Bethlehem, Pa.: Moravian Church in America, 1967).

Haydon, C. *Anti-Catholicism in eighteenth-century England. A political and social study* (Manchester & New York: Manchester University Press, 1993).

Heitzenrater, R.P. *Wesley and the people called Methodists* (Nashville, Tn.: Abingdon Press, 1995).

Hempton, D. *Methodism and Politics in British Society 1750–1850* (London: Hutchinson, 1984).

Hempton, D. 'Evangelicalism and reform c. 1780–1832'. In *Evangelical faith*, J. Wolffe (ed.), 17–37 (London: SPCK, 1995).

Hempton, D. *The Religion of the People. Methodism and popular religion, c. 1750–1900* (London & New York: Routledge, 1996).

Hempton, D. & M. Hill (eds) *Evangelical Protestantism in Ulster Society 1740–1890* (London and New York: Routledge, 1992).

Hilton, B. *The Age of Atonement: the influence of Evangelicalism on social and economic thought, 1795–1865* (Oxford: Clarendon Press, 1988).

Hindmarsh, D.B. *John Newton and the English Evangelical tradition: between the conversions of Wesley and Wilberforce* (Oxford: Oxford University Press, 1996).

Hole, R. *Pulpits, politics and public order in England 1760–1832* (Cambridge: Cambridge University Press, 1989).

Hutton, J.E. *A History of the Moravian Church* (London: Moravian Publication Office, 1909).

Hylson-Smith, K. *Evangelicals in the Church of England, 1734–1834* (Edinburgh: T. & T. Clark, 1989).

Hylson-Smith, K. *Churches in England from Elizabeth I to Elizabeth II*: Volume II 1689–1833 (London: SCM Press, 1997).

Jacob, W. *Lay People and Religion in the early eighteenth century* (Cambridge: Cambridge University Press, 1996).

Jacob, W.M. *Clergy and Society in Norfolk, 1707–1806*. PhD thesis, University of Oxford, 1982.

Jenkins, G.H. *Literature, religion and society in Wales, 1660–1730* (Cardiff: University of Wales Press, 1978).

Johnson, P. *Intellectuals* (London: Weidenfeld & Nicolson, 1988).

Jones, C (ed.). *Britain in the first age of party 1680–1750. Essays presented to Geoffrey Holmes* (London and Ronceverte: Hambledon Press, 1987).

Jones, G.F. *The Salzburger Saga. Religious exiles and other Germans along the Savannah* (Athens, Georgia: University of Georgia Press, 1984).

Knight, H.H. III *The Presence of God in the Christian Life: John Wesley and the Means of Grace* (Metuchen, N.J. & London: Scarecrow Press, 1992).

Knox, R.A. *Enthusiasm. A chapter in the history of Religion. With special reference to the XVII and XVIII centuries* (Oxford: Clarendon Press, 1950).

Landsman, N. 'Evangelists and their hearers: popular interpretation of revivalist preaching in eighteenth-century Scotland' *Journal of British Studies*, 28(2), 120–49, 1989.

Lewis, A.J. *Zinzendorf. The ecumenical pioneer. A study in the Moravian contribution to Christian Mission and Unity* (London: SCM Press, 1962).

Lewis, D. *Lighten their darkness: the Evangelical Mission to working class London, 1828–1860* (Westport, Conn: Greenwood Press, 1986).

Lewis, D.M. (ed.) *The Blackwell Dictionary of Evangelical Biography* [2 volumes] (Oxford & Cambridge, Mass: Blackwell, 1995).

Lovegrove, D. *Established Church, sectarian people. Itinerancy and the transformation of English Dissent 1780–1830* (Cambridge: Cambridge University Press, 1988).

Luker, D. 'Revivalism in theory and practice: the case of Cornish Methodism' *Journal of Ecclesiastical History*, 37(4), 603–19, 1986.

McLoughlin, W.G. *Revivals, awakenings and reform: an essay on religion and social change in America, 1607–1977* (Chicago: Chicago University Press, 1978).

Martin, R.H. *Evangelicals United: Ecumenical Stirrings in pre-Victorian Britain, 1795–1830* (Metuchen, N.J. & London: Scarecrow Press, 1983).

Marsden, G. (ed.) *Evangelicalism and Modern America* (Grand Rapids: William B. Eerdmans Publishing Company, 1984).

Marsden, G. *Religion and American Culture* (Orlando, Florida: Harcourt Brace College Publishers, 1990).

Mather, F.C. 'Georgian Churchmanship reconsidered: some variations in Anglican public worship 1714–1830' *Journal of Ecclesiastical History*, 36(2), 255–83, 1985.

Milburn, G. & M. Batty *Workaday Preachers. The story of Methodist local preaching* (London: Methodist Publishing House, 1995).

*Moravian Almanac. Daily Watchwords 1997: The Moravian Textbook with Almanac* (London: Moravian Book Room, 1997).

Murray, J. 'Gender attitudes and the contribution of women to evangelism and ministry in the nineteenth century'. In *Evangelical faith*, J. Wolffe (ed.), 97–116 (London: SPCK, 1995).

Newport, K.G.C. 'Methodists and the Millennium: eschatological expectation and the interpretation of Biblical prophecy in early British Methodism'. *Bulletin of the John Rylands University Library of Manchester* 78(1), 103–22, 1996.

Noll, M., D.W. Bebbington & G.A. Rawlyk (eds) *Evangelicalism. Comparative studies of popular Protestantism in North America, the British Isles and beyond, 1700–1990* (New York & Oxford: Oxford University Press, 1994).

Nuttall, G. 'Methodism and the older Dissent: some perspectives'. *Journal of the United Reformed Church History Society* 2(8), 259–74, 1981.

Obelkevich, J. *Religion and rural society: South Lindsey 1825–1875* (Oxford: Clarendon Press, 1976).

O'Brien, P. 'Agriculture and the home market for English industry, 1660–1820' *English Historical Review* 100(2) 773–99, 1985.

O'Brien, S. 'Eighteenth-century publishing networks in the first years of transatlantic evangelicalism'. (See Noll, Bebbington & Rawlyk, 38–57, 1994).

O'Gorman, F. *Voters, patrons and parties: the unreformed electoral system of Hanoverian England, 1734–1832* (Oxford: Clarendon Press, 1989).

Overton, J.H. & F. Relton *The English Church from the Accession of George I to the end of the eighteenth century* (London: Macmillan, 1906).

Phillips, J.A. *Electoral Behavior in unreformed England. Plumpers, splitters and straights* (Princeton: Princeton University Press, 1982).

Podmore, C. 'The Bishops and the Brethren: Anglican attitudes to the Moravians in the mid-eighteenth century' *Journal of Ecclesiastical History* 41(4) 622–46, 1990.

Podmore, C. *The role of the Moravian Church in England: 1728-1760* D.Phil. thesis, University of Oxford, 1994.

Pollock, J. *Wilberforce* (London: Constable, 1977).

Porter, H.C. (ed.) *Puritanism in Tudor England* (London: Macmillan, 1970).

Rack, H.D. *Reasonable enthusiast. John Wesley and the rise of Methodism* (London: Epworth Press, 1989).

Reynolds, J.S. *The Evangelicals at Oxford, 1735–1871. A Record of an unchronicled movement* (Abingdon: Marcham Manor Press, 1975).

Robbins, K. (ed.) *Protestant Evangelicalism: Britain, Ireland, Germany and America, c.1750–c.1950* (Oxford: Blackwell, 1990).

Rosman, D.M. *Evangelicals and Culture* (London: Croom Helm, 1984).

Roxburgh, K.B.E. 'The Scottish Evangelical Awakening of 1742 and the religious societies'. *Journal of the United Reformed Church Historical Society* 5(5), 266–73, 1994.

Schmidt, L.E. *Holy Fairs: Scottish Communions and American Revivals in the early modern period* (Princeton, NJ: Princeton University Press, 1990).

Smith, M. *Religion in industrial society. Oldham and Saddleworth 1740–1865* (Oxford: Clarendon Press, 1994).

Smout, T.C. 'Born again at Cambuslang. New evidence on popular religion and literacy in eighteenth-century Scotland'. *Past & Present*, 97, 114–27, 1982.

Spurr, J. 'The Church, the societies and the moral revolution of 1688'. (See Walsh, Haydon & Taylor, 127–42, 1993).

Storch, R.D. (ed.) *Popular culture and custom in nineteenth-century England* (London: Croom Helm, 1982).

Stout, H.S. *The Divine Dramatist: George Whitefield and the rise of modern evangelicalism* (Grand Rapids: Eerdmans, 1991).

Stout, H.S. 'George Whitefield in three countries'. (See Noll, Bebbington & Rawlyk, 58–72, 1994).

Sykes, N. *Church and State in England in the XVIII Century* (Cambridge: Cambridge University Press, 1934).

Taylor, S. 'William Warburton and the Alliance of Church and State'. *Journal of Ecclesiastical History*, 43(2), 271–86, 1992.

Thompson, D.M. *Denominationalism and Dissent, 1795–1835: a question of identity* (London: Dr Williams's Trust, 1985).

Thompson, E.P. *The Making of the English Working Class* (London: Gollancz, 1963).

Towlson, C.W. *Moravian and Methodist. Relationships and influences in the eighteenth century* (London: Epworth Press, 1957).

Tyerman, L. *The Life and Times of the Rev. John Wesley, M.A.* [2 volumes] (London: Hodder & Stoughton, 1870–71).

Urdank, A.M. *Religion and Society in a Cotswold Vale. Nailsworth, Gloucestershire, 1780–1865* (Berkeley: University of California Press, 1990).

Valenze, D.M. *Prophetic sons and daughters. Female preaching and popular religion in industrial England* (Princeton: Princeton University Press, 1985).

Vickery, A. 'Golden age to separate spheres?' *Historical Journal* 36(2), 383–414, 1993.

Virgin, P. *The Church in an age of negligence 1700–1840. Ecclesiastical structure and problems of Church reform 1700–1840* (Cambridge: James Clarke, 1989).

Virgin, P. *Sydney Smith* (London: HarperCollins, 1994).

Walsh, J. 'Methodism at the end of the eighteenth century'. In *A History of the Methodist Church in Great Britain*, G. Rupp & R. Davies (eds), 277–315 (London: Epworth, 1965).

Walsh, J. 'Origins of the Evangelical Revival'. In *Essays in Modern English Church History. In Memory of Norman Sykes* (London: A. & C. Black, 1966).

Walsh, J. 'Elie Halévy and the Birth of Methodism'. *Transactions of the Royal Historical Society*, 5th series, 25, 1–20, 1975.

Walsh, J. 'Religious Societies: Methodist and Evangelical 1738–1800'. In *Voluntary Religion*, W.J. Sheils and D. Wood (eds), 279–302 (Oxford: Blackwell, 1986).

Walsh, J. 'John Wesley and the community of goods'. (See Robbins, 25–50, 1990).

Walsh, J. *John Wesley, 1703–1791: A bicentennial tribute* (London: Dr Williams's Trust, 1994).

Walsh, J. 'Calvinism in the Church of England, c.1730–c.1830'. Unpublished paper, Jesus College, Oxford, 1997.

Walsh, J., C. Haydon & S. Taylor (eds) *The Church of England, c.1689–c.1833. From Toleration to Tractarianism* (Cambridge: Cambridge University Press, 1993).

Walvin, J. 'The rise of British popular sentiment for abolition, 1787–1832'. In *Anti-Slavery, Religion and Reform. Essays in Memory of Roger Anstey* (Folkestone & Hamden, Conn.; Dawson & Archon, 1980).

Ward, W.R. 'Power and Piety: the origins of religious revival in the early eighteenth century'. *Bulletin of the John Rylands University Library of Manchester* 63, 231–52, 1980.

Ward, W.R. *The Protestant Evangelical Awakening* (Cambridge: Cambridge University Press, 1992).

Warne, A. *Church and Society in Eighteenth-Century Devon* (Newton Abbot: David & Charles, 1969).

Watts, M.R. *The Dissenters. I. From the Reformation to the French Revolution* (Oxford: Clarendon Press, 1978).

Watts, M.R. *The Dissenters. II. The expansion of evangelical Nonconformity* (Oxford: Clarendon Press, 1995).

Wearmouth, R.F. *Methodism and the working-class movements of England 1800–1850* (London: Epworth, 1937).

Welch, E. *Spiritual Pilgrim. A reassessment of the life of the Countess of Huntingdon* (Cardiff: University of Wales Press, 1995).

Wesley, J. *Journals* In *Wesley and the people called Methodists*, Heitzenrater, R.P. (ed.) (Nashville, Tn.: Abingdon Press, 1995).

Wolffe, J. 'Catholicism and Evangelical Identity in Britain and the United States, 1830–1860'. (See Noll, Bebbington & Rawlyk, 179–97, 1994).

Wolffe, J. (ed.) *Evangelical faith and public zeal. Evangelicals and society in Britain 1780–1980* (London: SPCK, 1995b).

Young, D. *The origin and history of Methodism in Wales and the borders* (London: Charles H. Kelly, 1893).

# Index

activism 26, 29–30, 54
Age of Reason 32–4, 45
American Protestant Society 112
Anstey, Roger 108–9
antinomianism 69, 118
Arianism 33, 34, 51, 54, 118
Arminianism 23, 27–9, 68, 71–3, 75, 79, 83, 91, 99, 104, 107–9, 114, 118
Atkinson, Christopher 47
atonement doctrine 27–8, 33
Atterbury, Francis 25
authority, evangelicalism and 78–97

Bagshawe, William 38, 55
baptismal regeneration 32, 36
Baptists 35, 87, 90, 93–4, 99, 101
Barritt, Mary 103
Baskerville, S. W. 41
Batty, M. 2
Baxter, Richard 38
Bebbington, D. W. 1, 26, 28, 30, 31, 113
Bengel, Johannes Albrecht 15
Benson, Joseph 104
Benson, Martin, Bishop of Gloucester 58
Berridge, John 73
Betham-Edwards, M. 29

Bible/biblicism 2, 14–15, 25–7, 29, 33, 35–6, 46–7, 49–50, 100–1
biographical approach 5–6
Black J. 99, 100
Bohemia/Bohemian church 16–17
Böhler, Peter 20, 60
Bolam, C. G. 55
Book of Common Prayer 37
Bourne, Hugh 85
Boynton, L. 46
Bradburn, Samuel 84
Bray, Thomas, Rector of Sheldon 35
Britain 4, 24–38
    existing churches 39–56
British and Foreign Bible Society 94
Brown, Ford K. 105
Brown, S. J. 91, 92
Browne, Robert 30
Buckley, James 28
Bunting, Jabez 88
Burke, Edmund 83, 100

Calvin, John 71, 118
Calvinism 23, 27, 115, 118
    authority 88, 90–4, 97
    in Britain 27, 45–6, 48–9, 51–2, 54
    controversy 68, 71–3
    impact of revival 99, 106–8
Cambuslang 53, 54, 91

Carwardine, R. J. 104, 110, 114
Catholicism 10–11, 13, 17, 66–7, 73,
    89, 93, 98, 102, 107, 111–12
Cennick, John 28, 30, 51, 61, 68–71,
    75, 101
Chalmers, Thomas 91–2
charity schools 35, 50, 65
Charles, Thomas 94
Chauncy, Charles 23
Cheshunt College 116–17
Chilcote, P. W. 103
Chillingworth, William 26–7
'Christian perfection' 72
Christie, I. R. 82
chronological approach 4–5
Church of England 1, 7, 33–4, 64,
    102, 105–7
    authority of evangelicalism 78–9,
        81, 84–5, 88, 90, 94–5, 97
    evangelical revival and 39–56
Church of Ireland 50–2, 93
Church Missionary Society 94
Church of Scotland 51–4, 79, 92
Clapham Sect 48, 100, 107
Clark, J. C. D. 41, 82–3
Clarkson, Thomas 109
Clayton, John 47, 66
Clegg, James 38, 55
Clifford, A. C. 71
Clowes, William 85
de Coetlogon, Charles Edward 48, 73
Coke, Thomas 79, 81, 95
Colley, Linda 4
Comenius, Johannes Amos 17–18
Commonwealth period 54, 83
Congregationalism 4, 87, 90, 101
'Connexion' 62, 64, 79, 83, 88, 90
conversionism 21–3, 26, 28–31, 46–
    50, 55, 75–7, 113
Convocation 40, 41
Cooper, J. H. 28, 30, 69, 75
Corporation Act 40, 67
Council of Constance 17
Counter-Reformation 10, 19

Covenanters 52, 118–19
Cowper, William 101
Crawford, M. J. 21
Crosby, Sarah 103
Cross, F. L. 2
Crouch, Isaac 106
crucicentrism 26, 27–8
'cultural imperialism' 116
Currie, R. 64, 83–4, 86, 91

Davidoff, L. 105
Davidson, Margaret 103
Davie, Donald 55
Davies, Owen 77
Davis, R. W. 96
Davis, Richard 55
Declaratory Act (1719) 51
Deed of Declaration (1784) 79
Deism/Deists 33–4, 119
Denny, Lady Arabella 48
denominational approach 6–7
Dickinson, Elizabeth 103
Diderot, Denis 32
Dissenters 22, 33–5, 42, 44–5, 49, 51,
    54–6, 60, 66, 73, 78–9, 84, 87–90,
    93, 95–7
Doddridge, Philip 55, 65
Dow, Lorenzo 85
Dutch Reformed Church 21, 71
Dutton, Anne 104
Dutton, Benjamin 56

East India Company 94, 115
Edict of Nantes 10, 16
Edwards, Jonathan 4, 9, 21–4, 28, 31,
    52–3
Ellis, Rev. Edward 49
Ellis, K. L. 100
Elwin, M. 74
England 4, 93–7
enlightenment beliefs 31–2
Episcopalian Church 35, 52, 79
Erskine, Ebenezer 52, 53
erastianism 41

Europe 9–20
Evangelical Alliance 112
Evangelical History Society 2
*Evangelical Magazine* 99, 104
Evans, E. J. 43

Farley, Felix 99
Fawcett, A. 53
Fetter Lane Society 60, 69–70
Field, C. D. 65, 101
Finney, Charles 113
Fleming, Caleb 73–4
Fletcher, John 72–3
Fox, Charles James 90
Francis, Benjamin 91
Francke, August Hermann 12–16, 18,
    39–40
Frelinghuysen, Theodorus Jacobus
    21
Frémont, John C. 110
French Revolution 80–2, 89, 95, 98,
    100
Frend, William 107
Fuller, Andrew 94
fundamentalism 2–3

Gally, Rev. Henry 41
Gambold, John 46–7
geographical approach 3–4
Geyer-Kordesch, J. 14
Gibson, D. 45
Gibson, Edmund 73
Gibson, W. 106
Gilbert, A. D. 63–4, 83–4, 86–9,
    90–1
Gillespie, Thomas 54
Gladstone, W. E. 108
Goen, C. G. 22, 23, 28
Goring, H. L. 55
Great Awakening 22, 23
Gregory, J. 44
Grenville, Lord 95
Grimshaw, William 43
Guyse, John 22–3

Habsburgs 10, 13, 15, 16, 19
Halévy, Elie 65–6, 81–4, 86, 89, 95,
    105
Hall, C. 105
Hall, James 29, 75
Halle 13–14, 16, 53
Hanoverians 13, 77, 98
Hardie, Keir 115
Harris, Howell 9, 50, 58, 61, 64, 75
Hastings, Lady Betty 48
Hempton, D. 48, 75, 83, 89, 92–3,
    101–2, 104, 111
Henderson, Arthur 115
Herrnhut 18–19, 68, 103
Hervey, James 47
High Church 37, 54, 61, 83, 110
Hill, John 90–1
Hill, M. 48, 75, 93
Hoadly, Benjamin 41
Hone, Nathaniel 62
Horneck, Anthony 36
Horsley, L. 64, 83–4, 86, 91
Horsley, Samuel, Bishop of
    Rochester 96
Hotham, Lady Gertrude 48
Huguenots 10, 13, 16, 24, 48
Huntingdon, Selina Hastings,
    Countess of 6, 48–9, 62, 65, 67,
    72–3, 79, 116
Hurrell, Elizabeth 103
Hus, John 17
Hutton, J. E. 18, 60, 68–9

Ingham, Benjamin 47, 48, 62, 68
Ireland 4, 50–2, 82–3, 92–3, 103, 111

Jacob, W. 95
Jacobinism 81, 100
Jacobitism 11, 52, 66–7, 73, 98
Jenkins, Geraint H. 49–50, 66
Johnson, Paul 31–2
Johnson, Dr Samuel 25, 28, 38, 43,
    57, 59, 63, 73, 100
Jones, G. F. 19

Jones, Rev. Griffith 49
justification 25, 26, 45, 69, 119

Kilham, Alexander 85, 99
Kinchin, Charles 47
Knapp, L. M. 40
Knight, H. H. 71

Landsman, N. 101
latitudinarianism 41, 119
La Trobe, Benjamin 33
Lavington, George 73, 80, 102
Law, William 37
Lewis, A. J. 7, 16
Lewis, D. M. 63
Lewis, Sinclair 3
Lewis, W. S. 6
Livingstone, E. A. 2
London Corresponding Society 81, 84
London Missionary Society 94, 105
Lovegrove, D. 83, 87, 90–1, 94
Luker, D. 68, 87, 113
Luther, Martin 11, 26, 27
Lutheran Church 11–14, 39–40

McCulloch, William 53–4, 91, 92
Magdalene Chapel (Dublin) 48
Mant, Richard 83
Martyn, Henry 115
Mather, Alexander 79
Mather, F. C. 43, 44
Maxfield, Thomas 72
Mendham, Joseph 106–7, 112
Methodism 6–7, 20, 22, 113
    authority/legal status 78–97
    Britain 26–9, 37–8, 41–7, 49–51, 55–6
    growth of 57–77
    Primitive 85–8, 92
    Wesleyan 85–8, 91–3, 95, 107, 114–15
    women's role 101–5
Methodist Missionary Society 94

Milbanke, Judith 74
Milburn, G. 2
millenarianism 15, 102, 119
Milner, Isaac 107
missionary societies 93, 94, 105, 115–16
Mist, Nathaniel 45
Molther, Philipp Heinrich 69
Moorfields Tabernacle 49
'moral economy' 66, 82
morality 21, 31–2, 36–7, 45, 108, 110
Moravians 7, 16–20, 24, 33, 47–8, 60–1, 65, 67–70, 80, 87–8, 103, 116
More, Hannah 100, 107
Mortmain Act 67
Murphy, William 111
Murray, J. 104

Nelson, John 74
'New Birth' 11, 12, 29, 58
New Connection 85–8, 93, 99, 103
New England 21, 22–3, 52–3
Newton, John 73, 100, 101
non–jurors 37, 60, 119–20
non–residence 42–4, 64
Nonconformity 7, 33, 35, 37, 54, 56, 90
North, Lord 95, 108
Nuttall, Dr G. F. 55–6

O'Brien, P. 66, 82
O'Brien, Susan 20, 21
Oglethorpe, James 65
O'Gorman, Frank 90
original sin 25–6, 32–3, 54, 58, 71, 120
Overton, J. H. 43
Oxford Holy Club 7, 46–7, 50, 57, 58, 60, 62

Paine, Thomas 84, 100
Palatinate of the Rhine 16, 51
Palmer, John 91
patronage 48–9, 53, 65, 91, 107
Pawson, John 84

Percival, Spencer 107–8
Perronet, Edward 101
Perronet, Vincent 47, 48
Phillips, J. A. 90
Pietism 11–16, 18, 19, 37, 39, 52
Pitt the Younger, William 95, 96,
    108
Podmore, C. 33, 69, 70
politics 88–90, 94–7, 104, 108–12
Porteus, Beilby 106
Porter, H. C. 30
Potter, Archbishop 70
prayer societies 52–3
Presbyterianism 20, 35, 37, 51–2, 54–
    6, 91–3, 118–19
Priestley, Joseph 89
print culture 20–1, 29, 35, 45, 49–50,
    52, 54, 98–100, 102
Proclamation Society 110
Protestantism
    British context 24–7, 30, 45, 50–1
    impact of evangelicalism 98, 102,
        110–12
    international context 10–21
Puritanism 12, 20, 30, 37–8, 61, 81

Quakers 35, 87–8, 93, 103, 109

Rack, H. D. 46, 62, 83, 84
Raikes, Robert 100
Ranters 74, 120
'rational' religion 32–4, 45
Reformation 10, 11, 15, 20, 26, 30, 31,
    45–6, 112
religious societies 52–4, 58, 65, 101
Relton, F. 43
Restoration 45, 54
Reynolds, J. S. 106
Riland, John 48, 106–7
Romaine, William 47, 48
Ross, John 80
Rowland, Daniel 50, 58, 64
Roxburgh, K. B. E. 54
Rundle, Thomas 41, 42

Ryder, Henry, Bishop of Gloucester
    106

Sacheverell, Henry 66
Salzburgers 16, 19, 24
Scotland 4, 51, 52–4, 79, 91–2
Scott, Thomas 31, 34, 91
Seditious Meetings Act (1795) 96
Semmel, Bernard 114
'separate spheres' doctrine 104,
    105
Seward, William 75
Shakers 102
Sidmouth, Lord 4, 96–7, 100
Simeon, Charles 93–4, 107
slave trade 108–10
Smith, Sydney 110
Smollett, Tobias 40
Smout, T. C. 53
Smythies, William 36
Society for Constitutional
    Information 84
Society for Promoting Christian
    Knowledge (SPCK) 35, 50
Society for the Propagation of the
    Gospel in Foreign Parts 35, 59,
    60
Society for the Suppression of Vice
    110
Socinianism 33–4, 120
Southcott, Joanna 102
Spener, Philipp Jakob 11–12, 13,
    16
Spurr, J. 36
Stanhope, Lord 42
'stillness controversy' 69–70
Stockdale, J. 75–6
Stoddard, Solomon 21
Stout, Harry S. 30
Sunday Schools 86, 89, 100
Sykes, Norman 43

Taft, Zechariah 6, 103
Taylor, Dan 99

Taylor, David 49, 62
Taylor, Michael Angelo 96
temperance movement 115
Tennent, William 52
Teschen 15, 18
Test Acts 40, 42, 67
Thirty Years War 10, 13, 17
Thompson, E. P. 86–7, 89
Thomson, George 47
Tillotson, John 45
Told, Silas 75, 77, 109–10
Toleration Act (1689) 35, 78, 79, 95, 96
Tories 66, 78, 98, 108, 111–12, 114
trinitarianism 34, 51, 54, 55
Trip, Ann 103
tropus 70, 120

Unitarians 89, 93, 107, 108, 109, 120
'Unitas Fratrum' 17–18
United States 19–23, 110, 112
Urdank, A. M. 91

Venn, Henry 33, 34, 37, 45, 47–8, 73, 94, 106–7
Venn, John 107
Vickery, A. 105
Virgin, P. 44
voluntary activity 35–7

Wade, John 42–3
Wake, William 70
Wales 4, 49–50, 51, 58, 91
Walker, Samuel 75
Walpole, Horace 6
Walpole, Sir Robert 42, 66–8
Walsh, J. 20, 25, 34–7, 47, 56, 68, 84–5, 94, 99
Walvin, J. 110
Warburton, William 40, 41
Ward, W. R. 3–4, 9–12, 14–15, 19, 23, 29, 53, 88

Warmington, William 80–1
Warne, A. 43
Watts, Isaac 22, 55
Watts, M. R. 58, 65, 81, 84, 85, 90, 96
Wearmouth, R. F. 89
Welch, E. 48, 49, 67, 68, 116
Wesley, Charles 9, 19, 29, 36, 46–7, 58–60, 78, 101
Wesley, John 3–6, 9, 15, 19–20, 99, 104, 116, 118
  authority relations 78–81, 84–5, 91, 95
  and British evangelicalism 25–6, 30, 32–3, 36, 37, 41, 46–7, 49, 51
  growth of Methodism 57–64, 66–75
Wesley, Susannah 102
Whigs 40–2, 66, 67, 90, 94–6, 98, 109–10
Whitefield, George 5, 6, 9, 19–20, 22, 30, 37, 46–7, 49, 53, 58–9, 61–5, 72, 74, 79–80, 90
Whitehead, John 5–6, 95
Whitelamb, John 47
Wilberforce, William 36, 91, 100, 107–11
Williams, Joseph 55
Wilson, Thomas 80
Wolffe, J. 112
women 6, 7–8, 48–9, 63, 65, 74, 101–5
Woodforde, James 57
Woodward, George 44, 110
Woodward, Josiah 36
Wymondesold, Mr 44–5

Young, Arthur 29
Young, D. 49

Zinzendorf, Count von 7, 9, 16, 18–19, 29–30, 60, 70, 101, 120